Examples to Accompany
Descriptive Cataloging of Rare Books
2nd Edition

Prepared by the
Bibliographic Standards Committee
of the
Rare Books and Manuscripts Section

Association of College and Research Libraries
A division of the American Library Association
Chicago 1999

The paper used in this publication meets the minimum requirements of American National Standard for Information Sciences–Permanence of Paper for Printed Library Materials, ANSI Z39.48-1992. ∞

Library of Congress Cataloging-in-Publication Data
Examples to accompany Descriptive cataloging of rare books / prepared
    by the Bibliographic Standards Committee of the Rare Books and
    Manuscripts Section (ACRL/ALA)
        p. cm.
    Includes bibliographical references (p.   ) and index.
    ISBN 0-8389-8014-7 (alk. paper)
    1. Cataloging of rare books--Problems, exercises, etc. 2. Anglo
-American cataloguing rules. 3. Descriptive cataloging--United
States--Problems, exercises, etc. I. Association of College and
Research Libraries. Rare Books and Manuscripts Section.
Bibliographic Standards Committee. II. Descriptive cataloging of
rare books.
Z695.74.U54 1991 Suppl. 1999
025.3'416--dc21   99-24577

Printed in the United States of America.

03 02 01 00 99   5 4 3 2 1

INTRODUCTION

Purpose and Audience

Examples to Accompany Descriptive Cataloging of Rare Books is intended to be used with *Descriptive Cataloging of Rare Books*, 2nd ed. (Washington, D.C.: Cataloging Distribution Service, Library of Congress, 1991) (*DCRB*) as an illustrative aid to catalogers and others interested in or needing to interpret rare book cataloging. As such, it is to be used in conjunction with the rules it illustrates, both in *DCRB* and in *AACR2*, and in the context of local institutional practice.

Examples are particularly useful in rare book cataloging because of the complexity of many rare books and their corresponding catalog records. The variations in printing practices, lack of standardized title pages in early works, range of languages, and the artifactual aspects of rare books can all pose problems for the cataloger. Through use of examples, these potentially difficult areas can be clarified. In addition, the necessity of incorporating into rare book cataloging elements of other disciplines, such as descriptive bibliography, can be made easier for the cataloger by consulting examples as well as the appropriate manuals.

This publication is aimed at all who catalog rare books according to *DCRB*. It will be especially useful to the novice rare book cataloger and to the cataloger who catalogs rare books infrequently. We hope that it will also be an aid to experienced rare book catalogers who are confronted with unfamiliar bibliographical problems or materials out of their usual areas of expertise. Others who may find this handbook helpful are those who seek to interpret rare book cataloging, including special collections reference librarians and researchers. We expect that it will also serve the needs of educators and trainers of rare book catalogers, whether in library schools, workshops or actual work settings.

The examples in this handbook are illustrative and not prescriptive. They are meant as models rather than standards, and should never be seen as substitutes for the rules from which they are derived. Catalogers will need to use judgment in adopting or adapting these examples for use in their work. They will want to consider the needs of the users of their collections in the contexts of both local cataloging policy and national standards. Still, we hope that this publication will promote effective and consistent use of rare book cataloging standards by providing models that illustrate those standards.

Background

Examples to Accompany Descriptive Cataloging of Rare Books replaces the ten examples found on p. [55]-60 of *Bibliographic Description of Rare Books* (*BDRB*), the first edition of the rare book cataloging rules now known as *Descriptive Cataloging of Rare Books*. When *BDRB* was revised in 1990-91 by members of the Bibliographic Standards Committee and staff members from the Library of Congress, examples were omitted from the resulting publication, in large part due to time constraints. Surveys conducted during the revision of *BDRB* revealed that many catalogers wished for more, and more complete, examples. Since it was not possible to satisfy this need during the revision of the rules, the Bibliographic Standards Committee undertook a project to prepare a separate publication containing examples.

Work on the *Examples* began almost immediately after the publication of *DCRB*. A subcommittee of the Bibliographic Standards Committee prepared drafts of the *Examples* for discussion and revision at American Library Association meetings in 1992 and 1993. These drafts were based initially on the handbook developed by Suzy Taraba and Stephen R. Young for the Rare Book Cataloging class they taught at Columbia University's Rare Book School during the summers of 1986-91, and on Eric Holzenberg's handbook used in rare book cataloging workshops in the Chicago area. Other examples were solicited, primarily from other members and friends of the Bibliographic Standards Committee, to fill in gaps. No open solicitation for examples was conducted because of the difficulty of revising examples without the books in hand.

This revised edition of the *Examples* has been undertaken to address changes brought about by the integration of USMARC formats in 1995 and 1996, to correct errors discovered in the first edition, and to update fields, subfields and indicators made obsolete in the interim. Citations (510 fields) were corrected to conform to the 1996 second edition of *Standard Citation Forms for Published Bibliographies and Catalogs Used in Rare Book Cataloging (SCF)*. Also the bibliography following this introduction has been updated to include tools currently available via the internet.

INTRODUCTION

Scope

The aim of this publication is to illustrate *DCRB*, with special emphasis on those rules that are unusually complex, those that differ from *AACR2* and those that differ from *BDRB*. The examples encompass materials from a wide range of dates, places of publication and languages.

Two options receive special treatment. The option to record all original punctuation (*DCRB* rule 0E, p. 4) is illustrated by cataloging the same item twice (examples 26A and 26B), once using conventional and ISBD punctuation, and again using the original punctuation option, with resulting double punctuation. In similar fashion, the catalog record used to illustrate minimal-level cataloging appears in three versions (examples 40A, 40B and 40C), first as a full-level record, then as the briefest allowable minimal-level record, and finally as a minimal-level record with options applied. (See *DCRB*, Appendix D: Minimal-Level Records, p. 75-76; specifications for a *DCRB* "core" standard are under discussion as this publication goes to press.) Another option, that of recording graphic processes in the physical description area, is illustrated in examples 4, 23, 30 and 34.

Examples of records illustrating "special collections cataloging" (as defined in *DCRB*, Appendix E: *DCRB* Code for Records, p. 77) are excluded. In this context, "special collections cataloging" means fuller use of notes, access points, and other elements that are not specifically called for in *AACR2* or its predecessors, but that follow the spirit of *DCRB* without following its rules completely. The resulting records are too variable to be usefully illustrated.

The decision regarding when to use *DCRB*, "special collections cataloging," or *AACR2* is a matter of institutional policy. This handbook includes examples of fifteenth- through twentieth-century materials cataloged according to full *DCRB*. With a few exceptions (examples 18, a bound collection of pamphlets; 27, a single-sheet publication; and 44, a serial) all are monographic books or pamphlets, which constitute by far the largest part of the materials encountered by most rare book catalogers. In the last few years, however, catalogers have found that they are more and more concerned with serials; at the time of this writing a module for the cataloging of rare serials is being developed for the *CONSER Cataloging Manual*, in consultation with the Bibliographic Standards Committee. Brief guidelines based on Library of Congress practice are found in *DCRB* Appendix C: Rare Serials.

Since subject practice is not covered in descriptive cataloging codes such as *DCRB* and *AACR2*, and is essentially the same for rare books as for other materials, the Committee decided for reasons of space that subject headings could be omitted from the examples without diminishing the usefulness of the publication.

Arrangement and Format of Examples

The examples in this handbook are arranged chronologically by the date of publication of the item cataloged. This arrangement is supplemented by title, author, rule number and topical indexes.

Each example includes a reproduction of the title page (or title page substitute) of the item cataloged, printed on the page facing the record to allow for convenient comparison. Some examples also include reproductions of other relevant parts of the item, such as the colophon or a text sample used to determine proper transcription of early letter forms.

MARC-coded records are used, in recognition of the fact that most catalogers now prepare catalog records for an online database rather than a manual card catalog. Each is a "generic" USMARC record with full tagging for record-level variable fields. The form of tagging used is neither OCLC- nor RLIN-based, nor does it reflect the practice of any of the other major utilities or local online catalogs. Labels such as "Contents:" and "References:", which are generally system-supplied as "print constants" in an automated environment, do not appear in the examples, which are intended to represent the fields as input. Fixed fields are omitted, as are any variable fields that precede the main entry (1XX) field. (See *DCRB*, Appendix E: *DCRB* Code for Records, p. 77, for proper coding of MARC field 040.)

Conventions of modern punctuation are generally used in the examples. (See *DCRB* 0E, par. 5, p. 4). Appropriate modern punctuation is, to some extent, a matter of cataloger's judgment. The *Examples* follow *AACR2* prescribed punctuation, as well as some conventions that are used in *AACR2* but are not specifically prescribed, such as the practice of inserting commas before and after the word "or" (or its equivalent) that often signals an alternative title.

INTRODUCTION

Local Note Options, Local Added Entry Options and Copy-Specific Information

As we noted at the beginning of this introduction, "the examples in this handbook are illustrative and not prescriptive." This is especially so in the case of copy-specific or institution-specific information, as well as the use of "special" tracings and other tracings not specifically called for in *AACR2*. In fact, the editors of *DCRB* decided not to include an appendix, "Copy-Specific Data Elements," which described conventions followed by the Library of Congress. (As "Copy-Specific Data Elements for Rare Books" the text of the draft appendix was published in *Cataloging Service Bulletin* 53 (Summer 1991), p. 40-46). Still, it is hoped that the *Examples*—which differ in some points from LC practice—may be useful as a model to inform local policy. As in other areas, catalogers must follow the requirements of their bibliographic utilities and their local online catalogs.

For the sake of consistency, all copy-specific notes and added entries in the examples are given as USMARC fields with subfield 5, following the field definitions of *USMARC Format for Bibliographic Records*. Local practice, and/or that of the national bibliographic utility used by an institution, may dictate otherwise. For example, an institution may treat all local notes and added entries as 59X, 79X or other locally-defined fields; omit local elements when creating a master record for a utility, and add them locally only after the master record has been uploaded; or restrict provenance information to the local system.

The access points given in the examples include title tracings called for in *DCRB* Appendix A: Title Access Points (p. 67-68), thesaurus terms (655 field) from the thesauri prepared by the Bibliographic Standards Committee (see Bibliography), and some special tracings that might typically be used in a special collection library (printer, former owner, etc.). The cataloger's use of all these access points will depend on local policy. We have made no attempt to present all possible tracings, thesaurus terms, or special tracings for any given record.

All copy-specific fields in these examples, including those 655 fields that provide access to copy-specific aspects of an item, are highlighted by a vertical slash to the left of the field tag. Each of these fields ends with subfield 5, containing the USMARC code of the institution or organization that holds the copy to which the note or added entry applies, e.g. NcD (Duke University Library), DFo (Folger Library), InU-Li (Lilly Library). (This subfield was recently authorized for use in 655 fields. It is generally not required in fields that are local by definition, e.g. 59X, 79X). The authority for the codes is *Symbols of American Libraries*, maintained by the Library of Congress, which also includes codes for over 4000 Canadian Libraries and over 500 libraries in other countries. In the examples, a fill value "[INSTITUTION CODE]" has been supplied.

Annotation and Editorial Treatment of the Records

Below each catalog record are listed the principal *DCRB* rules used in its creation. Although the most significant rules associated with each example are given, it is impossible to cite in the available space every rule used by the cataloger of any given item. Some of the most basic rules (such as those governing transcription of early letter-forms) apply to virtually every situation encountered in rare book cataloging; these rules have been listed only where there are particularly clear examples of their use. However, the topical index will in most cases list every occurrence of such a rule, whether or not it has been cited in the rule list for a particular example. In all cases, when a rule includes an option, the primary rule, rather than the option, is illustrated unless otherwise stated.

In the lists, the *DCRB* numer for each rule is given, as well as a brief phrase that describes the topic of the rule and/or specific points or options which are illustrated. Each rule is assigned a reference number (in the column to the left), which will also be found to the left of each field that illustrates its use in the record. The reader can thus make the connection both ways, from example to rule and from rule to example.

Catalog records found in the *Examples* will necessarily vary from the records for the same items which appear in the national utilities or in local institutional catalogs. The records in the utilities and the catalogs have not been routinely updated to reflect the changes in cataloging codes. In preparing this handbook, the examples were edited for clarity, consistency and accuracy.

The *Examples* are drawn from real cataloging prepared by several rare book catalogers at a variety of institutions. Experienced catalogers realize that there is frequently more than one acceptable or appropriate way to solve a cataloging problem. Local policy may influence the way in which some rules are applied, individual interpretation of some rules can vary, and of course each cataloger brings different experience and judgment to the job. The Committee believes that the variety inherent in these examples accurately reflects the realities of rare book cataloging. By showing more than one solution to a given problem, we hope that the *Examples* will be more helpful to catalogers than would a strictly uniform approach to similar situations.

Corrections and Suggestions

Corrections, suggestions, and questions about *Examples to Accompany Descriptive Cataloging of Rare Books* should be directed to the RBMS Bibliographic Standards Committee. Any correspondence regarding this publication should be addressed to

> Chair, Bibliographic Standards Committee
> Rare Books and Manuscripts Section
> ACRL/ALA
> 50 East Huron Street
> Chicago IL 60611
>
> Attention: Handbook of Examples

Acknowledgments

This revision of the handbook was prepared by the Bibliographic Standards Committee of the Rare Books and Manuscripts Section of the Association of College and Research Libraries. The subcommittee charged with preparing draft documents was chaired by Melinda K. Hayes. Other members of the subcommittee were John Attig, Emily Epstein, Eric Holzenberg, Deborah J. Leslie, and Russell Martin. Other members of the Bibliographic Standards Committee during the work on this publication were Christine M. Clarke, Laurence Creider, Jane Gillis, Juliet McLaren, Robert L. Maxwell, Richard Noble, Henry Raine, Liz Robinson, Sandra Sider, Bruce Tabb, and Jerry Wager.

The subcommittee charged with preparing draft documents for the first edition of the handbook was first chaired by Suzy Taraba and later by Eric Holzenberg. Other members of the subcommittee were Elizabeth Herman, Nixie Miller, Eve Pasternak, and Jocelyn Sheppard. Other members of the Bibliographic Standards Committee during the work on the first edition were Laura Stalker (Chair), Virginia Bartow, Jain Fletcher, Elizabeth Johnson, Rita Lunnon, Deborah Ryszka, Joe Springer, and Belinda Urquiza.

Many catalogers prepared the records on which this publication is based. The cataloging of examples from Duke University was done by Nixie Miller, Dan Rettberg, Diane Shaw, and Suzy Taraba; from Loyola University by Eric Holzenberg; from Yale University by Cynthia Crooker, James Fox, and Stephen R. Young; from the Lilly Library by Steve Cape, Diane Bauerle, and Elizabeth Johnson; from the Folger Shakespeare Library by Henry Raine; from the Library Company of Philadelphia by Deborah J. Leslie. Librarians who contributed extensive comments include Elizabeth Herman (Getty Center), Brian Hillyard (National Library of Scotland), Elizabeth Johnson (Lilly Library), George Mullaly (University of Iowa), Eve Pasternak (Pierpont Morgan Library), Allen Poor (University of Chicago), Henry Raine (Folger Shakespeare Library), Patrick Russell (University of California, Berkeley), and Joe Springer (Goshen College). The topical index to the *Examples* is based on that prepared by David Rich (Brown University) for *DCRB*.

Significant institutional support for this project was given by Duke University, Loyola University, and the University of Southern California. In addition, many people in Perkins Library at Duke University provided invaluable assistance and technical support, including Dan Daily, Cheryl Gates, Sandra Hack Polaski, Glenda LaCoste, Greg Lyon, Diane Sutton, Cheryl Thomas, and Nelda Webb.

The Committee extends sincere thanks to all who helped make this project possible.

PHOTOGRAPHY CREDITS

Cover illustration: A woodcut of a scholar in his library from *Bocace des nobles maleureux* (Paris, 1538), a translation of Giovanni Boccaccio's *De casibus virorum illustrium*. Reproduced with permission of the Folger Shakespeare Library.

We are grateful to the following libraries for permission to reproduce items from their collections: Duke University, ex. 1, 3, 4, 7, 10, 12, 14, 16, 24, 25, 29, 31, 33, 34, 38, 40, 42, 45, 46; Folger Shakespeare Library, ex. 15, 18; Library Company of Philadelphia, ex. 47; Lilly Library, Indiana University, ex. 2, 39, 41, 43, 44, 48, 49; Loyola University of Chicago, ex. 6, 9, 11, 13, 17, 19-23, 26, 30, 32, 35, 50; Beinecke Library, Yale University, ex. 5, 8, 27, 28, 36, 37.

The Goff entries which appear as part of the illustration to ex. 1 are reproduced with the permission of the Kraus Reprint Company.

RARE BOOK CATALOGING TOOLS

Internet Resources

Many of the internet resources listed below under various categories, and many others not listed, are available via *RBMS Bibliographic Standards Committee Resources for the Rare Materials Cataloger*, maintained by Lawrence S. Creider, at <http://www.library.upenn.edu/ipc/index.html>. This is linked to the Bibliographic Standards Committee home page at <http://www.lib.byu.edu/~catalog/people/rlm/bsc/home.htm>, which in turn is linked to the RBMS home page at <http://www.princeton.edu/~ferguson/rbms.html>.

Cataloging Rules

Anglo-American Cataloguing Rules. 2nd ed. 1988 revision. Chicago: American Library Association, 1988.

CONSER Cataloging Manual. Jean L. Hirons, editor. Washington, D.C.: Serial Record Division, Library of Congress, 1983 (and updates).

CONSER Editing Guide. Prepared by the staff of the Serial Record Division under the direction of the CONSER Operations Coordinator. Washington, D.C.: Serial Record Division, Library of Congress, 1986 (and updates)

Descriptive Cataloging of Rare Books. 2nd ed. Washington, D.C.: Cataloging Distribution Service, Library of Congress, 1991. Included in the CD-ROM *Cataloger's Desktop*, available from the Cataloging Distribution Service. Also included in The Library Corporation's *Cataloger's Reference Shelf*, available for free via the Internet at <http://www.tlcdelivers.com/tlc/crs/rare0170.htm>.

ISBD(A): International Standard Bibliographic Description for Older Monographic Publications (Antiquarian). 2nd rev. ed. München; New York: Saur, 1991.

Thesauri, &c.

Binding Terms: A Thesaurus for Use in Rare Book and Special Collections Cataloguing. Prepared by the Bibliographic Standards Committee of the Rare Books and Manuscripts Section. Chicago: Association of College and Research Libraries, 1988.

Carter, John. *ABC for Book-Collectors*. 7th ed., with corrections, additions, and an introduction by Nicolas Barker. New Castle, Del.: Oak Knoll Books, 1995.

Genre Terms: A Thesaurus for Use in Rare Book and Special Collections Cataloguing. 2nd ed. Prepared by the Bibliographic Standards Committee of the Rare Books and Manuscripts Section. Chicago: Association of College and Research Libraries, 1991.

Paper Terms: A Thesaurus for Use in Rare Book and Special Collections Cataloguing. Prepared by the Bibliographic Standards Committee of the Rare Books and Manuscripts Section. Chicago: Association of College and Research Libraries, 1990.

Printing and Publishing Evidence: Thesauri for Use in Rare Book and Special Collections Cataloguing. Prepared by the Standards Committee of the Rare Books and Manuscripts Section. Chicago: Association of College and Research Libraries, 1986.

Provenance Evidence: Thesaurus for Use in Rare Book and Special Collections Cataloguing. Prepared by the Standards Committee of the Rare Books and Manuscripts Section. Chicago: Association of College and Research Libraries, 1988.

"Relator Terms for Rare Book, Manuscript, and Special Collections Cataloguing." Prepared by the Standards Committee of the Rare Books and Manuscripts Section. 3rd ed. *College & Research Libraries News,* v. 48, no. 9 (Oct. 1987), p. 553-557. [Supplemented by correction note on p. 645, v. 48, no. 10 (Nov. 1987)] The corresponding 3-letter codes for these terms are included in *USMARC Code List for Relators, Sources, Description Conventions.* 1987 ed. Washington, D.C.: Cataloging Distribution Service, Library of Congress, 1997.

Robert's and Etherington's Bookbinding and the Conservation of Books: a Dictionary of Descriptive Terminology, via the Internet by Walter Henry: <http://palimpsest.stanford.edu/don/don.html> [1994 version of out-of-print 1982 ed.]

Type Evidence: A Thesaurus for Use in Rare Book and Special Collections Cataloguing. Prepared by the Bibliographic Standards Committee of the Rare Books and Manuscripts Section. Chicago: Association of College and Research Libraries, 1990.

VanWingen, Peter M. and Belinda D. Urquiza. *Standard Citation Forms for Published Bibliographies and Catalogs Used in Rare Book Cataloging.* 2nd ed. Washington: Library of Congress, 1996; incorporating and modifying the supplement: "Citation Forms for Bibliographies Appearing in Journals or as Component Parts of Larger Works" Prepared by the Standards Committee of the Rare Books and Manuscripts Section. College & Research Libraries News, v. 49, no. 8 (Sept. 1988), p. 525-526.

Descriptive Bibliography

Bowers, Fredson T. *Principles of Bibliographical Description.* Princeton: Princeton University Press, 1949. [1994 reprint with new introd. by G. Thomas Tanselle. Winchester, U.K.: St. Paul's Bibliographies; New Castle, Del.: Oak Knoll Press]

Fingerprints = Empreintes = Impronte. Paris: Institut de Recherche et d'Histoire des Textes, 1984. Supplemented by: Nouvelles des empreintes = Fingerprint Newsletter (no. 1- 1981- Paris: Institut de Recherche et d'Histoire des Textes)

Gaskell, Philip. *A New Introduction to Bibliography.* Oxford: Clarendon Press, 1974 (c1972) [1995 reprint: Winchester, U.K.: St. Paul's Bibliographies; New Castle, Del.: Oak Knoll Press, 1995]

McKerrow, R. B. *An Introduction to Bibliography for Literary Students.* Oxford: Oxford University Press, 1965 (c1927) [1994 reprint: Winchester, U.K.: St. Paul's Bibliographies; New Castle, Del.: Oak Knoll Press, 1994]

Modern Forms of Latin Place Names

Grässe, Johann Georg Theodor. *Orbis Latinus: Lexicon lateinischer geographischer Namen des Mittelalters und der Neuzeit.*Grossausgabe, bearb. und hrsg. von Helmut Plechl unter Mitarbeit von Sophie-Charlotte Plechl. Braunschweig: Klinkhardt & Biermann, 1972.

Peddie, R. A. *Place Names in Imprints: An Index to the Latin and Other Forms Used on Title Pages.* London: Grafton & Co., 1932. [1968 reprint: Detroit: Gale Research Co.]

RBMS Bibliographic Standards Committee Latin Placenames File, via the Internet: <http://www.lib.byu.edu/~catalog/people/rlm/latin/names.htm> [names found in imprints of books published before 1801]

CATALOGING TOOLS

Abbreviations, Contractions, and Letter-Forms Used in Early Printing

Cappelli, Adriano. *Lexicon abbreviaturarum = Dizionario di abbreviature latine ed italiane usate nelle carte e codici specialmente del medio-evo* . . . 4. ed. Milano: Hoepli, 1949.

Cappelli, Adriano. *The Elements of Abbreviation in Medieval Latin Paleography.* Translated by David Heimann and Richard Kay. Lawrence, Kansas: University of Kansas Libraries, 1982. [translation of Cappelli's introduction to the Lexicon Abbreviaturarum]

McKerrow, R. B. "Some Notes on the Letters I, J, U and V in sixteenth-Century Printing." *The Library,* 3rd series, no. 1 (1910)

Chronology

The Book of Calendars. Frank Parise, editor. New York: Facts on File, 1982.

Calendar Conversions, via the Internet: <http://genealogy.org/~scottlee/calconvert.cgi>.

Cappelli, Adriano. *Cronologia, cronografia e calendario perpetuo, dal principio dell'èra cristiana ai nostri giorni.* 5. ed. aggiornata ed ampliata. Milano: Hoepli, 1983.

English Calendar, by Ian MacInnes, Albion College, via the Internet: <http://spider.albion.edu/fac/engl/calendar/>.

Pseudonyms and Anonyms

Barbier, A. A. *Dictionnaire des ouvrages anonymes.* 3e éd., rev. et augm. Paris: P. Daffis, 1872-1879. [1964 reprint: Paris: G. P. Maisonneuve & Larose]

Halkett, Samuel and John Laing. *Dictionary of Anonymous and Pseudonymous English Literature.* 3rd rev. and enl. ed., John Horden, editor. Harlow: Longman, 1980-

Holzmann, Michael and Hanns Bohatta. *Deutsches Anonymen-Lexicon, 1501-1850.* Weimar: Gesellschaft der Bibliophilen, 1902. [Reprints: Hildesheim: Olms, 1961; New York: Olms, 1984]

Medina, José Toribio. *Diccionario de anónimos y seudónimos hispanoamericanos.* Buenos Aires: Imprenta de la Universidad, 1925. [1973 reprint: Detroit: B. Etheridge]

Melzi, Gaetano. *Dizionario di opere anonime e pseudonime di scrittori italiani, o como che sia aventi relazione all'Italia.* Milano: L. di Giacomo Pirola, 1848-1859. [1960 reprint: New York: Burt Franklin]

Quérard, Joseph-Marie. *Les supercheries littéraires dévoilées.* 2. éd., considérablement augm., publiée par Gustave Brunet et Pierre Janet. Paris: P. Daffis, 1869-1870. [1960 reprint: Hildesheim: G. Olms]

False and Fictitious Imprints

Brunet, Gustave. *Imprimeurs imaginaires et libraires supposés.* Paris: Tross, 1866. [1963 reprint: New York: Burt Franklin]

Parenti, Marino. *Dizionario dei luoghi di stampa falsi, inventati o suppositi in opere di autori e traduttori italiani.* Firenze: Sansoni, 1951.

Weller, Emil Ottokar. *Die falschen und fingierten Druckorte*. 2. verm. und verb. Aufl. Leipzig: W. Engelmann, 1864. [1960 reprint: Hildesheim: Olms]

Woodfield, Denis B. *Surreptitious Printing in England, 1550-1640*. New York: Bibliographical Society of America, 1973.

Incunabula

Bibliothèque Nationale (France). *Catalogue des incunables*. Paris: Bibliothèque Nationale, 1981 [i.e. 1982-]

British Museum. Dept. of Printed Books. *Catalogue of Books Printed in the XVth Century Now in the British Museum*. London: Printed by order of the Trustees, 1908-1971.

Copinger, Walter Arthur. *Supplement to Hain's Repertorium Bibliographicum*. Berlin: J. Altmann, 1926. [1950 reprint: Milano: Görlich]

Gesamtkatalog der Wiegendrucke. *Herausgegeben von der Kommission für den Gesamtkatalog der Wiegendrucke*. Leipzig: K. W. Hiersemann, 1925- [Reprint: Stuttgart: A. Hiersemann; New York: H.P. Kraus, 1968-]

Goff, Frederick R. *Incunabula in American Libraries: A Third Census of Fifteenth-Century Books Recorded in North American Collections*. New York: Bibliographical Society of America, 1964. [1973 reprint: Millwood, N.Y.: Kraus Reprint Co.]

Hain, Ludwig Friedrich Theodor. *Repertorium Bibliographicum, in Quo Libri Omnes ab Arte Typographica Inventa usque ad Annum MD. Typis Expressi, Ordine Alphabetico vel Simpliciter Enumeratur vel Adcuratus Recensiter*. Stuttgart: J. G. Cotta, etc., 1826-1838. [1948 and 1966 reprint: Milano: Görlich]

Harvard University. Library. *A Catalogue of the Fifteenth-Century Printed Books in the Harvard University Library*. By James E. Walsh. Binghamton: CMERS, 1991-1994.

Incunabula Short-Title Catalogue. [Available through the RLIN or BLAISE databases]

Indice generale degli incunaboli delle biblioteche d'Italia. A cura del Centro Nazionale d'Informazioni Bibliografiche. Roma: Libreria dello Stato, 1943-1981.

Panzer, Georg Wolfgang Franz. *Annales Typographici ab Artis Inventae Origine ad Annum MD*. Nuremburg: J. B. Zeh, 1793-1803 [1963 reprint: Hildesheim: G. Olms]

Polain, Louis. *Catalogues des livres imprimés au quinzième siècle des bibliothèques de Belgique*. Bruxelles: Pour la Société des Bibliophiles & Iconophiles de Belgique, 1932.

Proctor, Robert. *An Index to the Early Printed Books in the British Museum: with Notes of Those in the Bodleian Library*. London: K. Paul, 1898-1903; B. Quaritch, 1938.

Reichling, Dietrich. *Appendices ad Hainii-Coperingeri Repertorium Bibliographicum*. Munich: I. Rosenthal, 1905-1911. [1953 reprint: Milano: Görlich]

CATALOGING TOOLS

General Bibliographies

British Museum. Dept. of Printed Books. *General Catalogue of Printed Books to 1955.* Photolithographic Edition. London: Trustees of the British Museum, 1959-1966.

Brunet, Jacques Charles. *Manuel du libraire et de l'amateur de livres.* 5 éd., originale entièrement refondue et augm. d'un tiers par l'auteur . . . Paris: Firmin Didot frères, fils et cie, 1860-1865 (and: Supplément. Par MM. P. Deschamps et G. Brunet, 1878-1880)

Grässe, Johann Georg Theodor. *Trésor de livres rares et précieux.* Berlin: J. Altmann, 1922.

Index Aureliensis: Catalogus Librorum Sedecimo Saeculo Impressorum. Editio princeps. Aureliae Aquensis, 1962-

Library of Congress, via the Internet: <http://lcweb.loc.gov/z3950/gateway.html#other> or <http://lcweb.loc.gov/catalog>

National Union Catalog, Pre-1956 Imprints: A Cumulative Author List Representing Library of Congress Printed Cards and Titles Reported by Other American Libraries. London: Mansell, 1968-1980 (and Supplement, 1980-1981)

Bibliothèque Nationale (France). Département des Imprimés. *Catalogue générale des livres imprimés de la Bibliothèque Nationale: Auteurs.* Paris: Impr. Nationale, 1897-

Bibliographies with a Geographic or Linguistic Focus

The Americas

Evans, Charles. *American Bibliography: A Chronological Dictionary of All Books, Pamphlets, and Periodical Publications Printed in the United States of America From the Genesis of Printing in 1639 Down to and Including the Year 1820.* Chicago: Privately printed for the author by the Blakely Press, 1903-1959. [reprints: New York: P. Smith, 1941-1959; Metuchen, N.J.: Mini-Print Corp., 1967]

Medina, José Toribio. *Biblioteca hispano-americana (1493-1810).* Santiago de Chile, 1898-1907. [1968 reprint: Amsterdam: L. Israel]

Sabin, Joseph. *A Dictionary of Books Relating to America, from its Discovery to the Present Time.* New York, 1868-1936. [Reprints: New York: Mini-Print Corp., 196-?; Metuchen, N.J.: Scarecrow Press, 1966]

Thompson, Lawrence Sidney. *The New Sabin: Books Described by Joseph Sabin and his Successors, Now Described Again on the Basis of Examination of Originals, and Fully Indexed by Title, Subject, Joint Authors, and Institutions and Agencies.* Troy, N.Y.: Whitston Pub. Co., 1974-

Belgium & Netherlands

British Library. *Catalogue of Books from the Low Countries 1601-1621 in the British Library.* Compiled by Anna E. C. Simoni. London: British Library, 1990.

British Museum. Dept. of Printed Books. *Short-Title Catalogue of Books Printed in the Netherlands and Belgium and of Dutch and Flemish Books Printed in Other Countries from 1470 to 1600 Now in the British Museum.* London: Trustees of the British Museum, 1965.

CATALOGING TOOLS

Europe

Adams, Herbert Mayow. *Catalogue of Books Printed on the Continent of Europe, 1501-1600, in Cambridge Libraries.* London: Cambridge University Press, 1967.

France

Baudrier, Henri Louis. *Bibliographie lyonnaise: recherches sur les imprimeurs, libraires, relieurs et fondeurs de lettres de Lyon au XVIe siècle.* Publiées et continuées par J. Baudrier. Lyon: Librairie Ancienne d'Auguste Brun, 1895-1921.

British Museum. Dept. of Printed Books. *Short-Title Catalogue of Books Printed in France and of French Books Printed in Other Countries from 1470 to 1600 Now in the British Museum.* London: Trustees of the British Museum, 1924 (and supplements)

Cioranescu, Alexandre. *Bibliographie de la littérature française du seizième siècle.* Collaboration et préface de V.-L. Saulnier. Paris: C. Klincksieck, 1959.

Cioranescu, Alexandre. *Bibliographie de la littérature française du dix-septième siècle.* Paris: Editions du Centre National de la Recherche Scientifique, 1965-1966.

Cioranescu, Alexandre. *Bibliographie de la littérature française du dix-huitième siècle.* Paris: Editions du Centre National de la Recherche Scientifique, 1969.

Goldsmith, Valentine Fernande. *A Short-Title Catalogue of French Books, 1601-1700, in the Library of the British Museum.* Folkestone: Dawsons, 1969-1973.

Germany

British Museum. Dept. of Printed Books. *Short-Title Catalogue of Books Printed in the German-Speaking Countries and German Books Printed in Other Countries from 1455-1600 Now in the British Museum.* London: Trustees of the British Museum, 1962.

Verzeichnis der im deutschen Sprachbereich erschienenen Drucke des XVI. Jahrhunderts: VD 16. Stuttgart: Hiersemann, 1983-

Great Britain

British Library. *The English Short-Title Catalogue (ESTC).* [available on microfiche, CD ROM, or through the RLIN or BLAISE databases]

Pollard, William and G. R. Redgrave. *A Short-Title Catalogue of Books Printed in England, Scotland, Ireland, and of English Books Printed Abroad, 1475-1640.* 2nd ed. London: Bibliographical Society, 1976-1991.

Wing, Donald Goddard. *Short-Title Catalogue of Books Printed in England, Scotland, Ireland, Wales, and British America and of English Books Printed in Other Countries, 1641-1700.* 2nd ed., rev. & enl. New York: Index Committee of the Modern Language Association, 1972-

Italy

British Library. *Catalogue of Seventeenth-Century Italian Books in the British Library.* London: The Library, 1986.

British Museum. Dept. of Printed Books. *Short-Title Catalogue of Books Printed in Italy and of Italian Books Printed in Other Countries from 1465 to 1600 Now in the British Museum.* London: Trustees of the British Museum, 1958.

Le edizioni italiane del XVI secolo: censimento nazionale. Roma: Istituto Centrale per il Catalogo Unico delle Biblioteche Italiane e per le Informazioni Bibliografiche, 1985-

Spain & Portugal

Biblioteca Nacional (Spain). *Catálogo general de incunables en bibliotecas españolas.* Madrid : Ministerio de Cultura, Direccion General del Libro y Bibliotecas, 1989-1994.

British Library. *Catalogue of Books Printed in Spain and of Spanish Books Printed Elsewhere in Europe Before 1601 Now in the British Library.* 2nd ed. London: British Library, 1989.

British Museum. Dept. of Printed Books. *Short-Title Catalogues of Spanish, Spanish-American and Portuguese Books Printed Before 1601 Now in the British Museum.* By H. Thomas. London: British Museum, 1966.

Haebler, Konrad. *Bibliografía ibérica del siglo XV: enumeración de todos los libros impresos en España y Portugal hasta el año de 1500.* La Haya: M. Nijhoff, 1903-1917 [1963 reprint: New York: B. Franklin]

Palau y Dulcet, Antonio. *Manual del librero hispano-americano: bibliografía general española e hispano-americana desde la invención de la imprenta hasta nuestros tiempos, con el valor comercial de los impresos descritos.* 2. ed. corr. y aumentada por el autor. Barcelona: A. Palau, 1948-1977.

Silva, Innocencio Francisco da. *Diccionário bibliographico portuguez.* Lisboa: Imprensa Nacional, 1858-1923. [1972 reprint]

Examples

A.

B. B-526 Biblia latina. [Mainz: Printer of the 42-
(B460) line Bible (Johann Gutenberg and Peter
Schoeffer?), about 1454-55, not after Aug.
1456.] f°. 42 ll.

C. B-607 — (cum glossa ordinaria Walafridi Stra-
(B541) bonis aliorumque et interlineari Anselmi
Laudunensis). [Strassburg: Adolf Rusch,
for Anton Koberger, not after 1480.] f°.

N.B: Apparently printed with types borrowed from
Johann Amerback — *cf* BMC I 92 or GW 4282.

EXAMPLE 1: A. First page of text **B.–C.** Goff entries B-526 and B-607 (source of supplied title)

EXAMPLE 1

CATALOG RECORD

ref. no.

	130 0	Bible. $l Latin. $s Vulgate. $f not after 1480.
1,2	245 10	[Biblia Latina : $b cum glossa ordinaria Walafridi Strabonis aliorumque et interlineari Anselmi Laudunensis]
2,3,4,5,6,7,8	260	[Strasbourg? : $b Adolf Rusch?, for Anton Koberger?, $c not after 1480]
9,10	300	4 v. ; $c 48 cm. (fol.)
11	500	Title from Goff.
12	500	Commonly thought to have been printed by Rusch with types borrowed from Johann Amerbach. Some authorities write that Amerbach printed this edition himself at Basel.
13	500	Printed in two columns of interlineated text surrounded by a glossary.
13	500	The signatures actually feature an irregular sequence of letters a-g (and perhaps h mixed with b), often repeating one letter through several gatherings (see BM Xvth, GW). Their purpose is not clear, but they may well have been intended to account for presswork, in the manner of the "press figures" found in many 18th-century English books.
14	510 4	BM 15th cent., $c I, p. 92
14	510 4	Copinger, W.A. Incunabula Biblica, $c 44
14	510 4	Goff $c B-607
14	510 4	GW $c 4282
14	510 4	Hain-Copinger $c 3173
14	510 4	Polain $c 682A
14	510 4	Proctor $c 299
15	500	Rubricated initials in red, blue and green. $5 [INSTITUTION CODE]
15	500	Library has v. 1 and 4; both vols. bound in blind-stamped half calf, paste paper over wooden boards, metal and leather clasps. $5 [INSTITUTION CODE]
15	500	Ms. note: Iste liber est canonicorum regularum monasterij Beat[a]e Virginis in [illegible]. $5 [INSTITUTION CODE]
	655 7	Signatures (Printing) $2 rbpri
	655 7	Signing patterns (Printing) $2 rbpri
	655 7	Clasps (Binding) $2 rbbin $5 [INSTITUTION CODE]
	655 7	Wooden boards (Binding) $2 rbbin $5 [INSTITUTION CODE]
	655 7	Paste papers (Paper) $2 rbpap $5 [INSTITUTION CODE]
	700 0	Walahfrid Strabo, $d 807?-849.
	700 0	Anselmus, $c of Laon, $d d. 1117.
	700 1	Rusch, Adolf, $d fl. 1466-1489, $e printer.
	700 1	Koberger, Anton, $d ca. 1440-1513, $e bookseller.
	700 1	Amerbach, Johannes, $d 1441?-1513, $e printer.
	752	France $d Strasbourg

PRINCIPAL *DCRB* RULES ILLUSTRATED

ref. no.

1	0C3	(no title page; title supplied from reference source)
2	0E, par. 9	(interpolations)
3	4A2	(publication information based on several reference sources)
4	4B1	(supplied place of publication given in English form)
5	4B12	(probable place of publication supplied from reference source)
6	4C1	(publisher statement includes printer)
7	4C8	(probable publisher supplied from reference source)
8	4D6	(date uncertain; "terminal date" pattern used)
9	5B16	(Publication in more than one physical unit)
10	5D1, par. 3	(format)
11	7C3	(source of title proper note)
12	7C8	(publication note)
13	7C10	(physical description note)
14	7C14	(references to published descriptions; required for incunabula)
15	7C18	(copy-specific note) See Introduction regarding Local Note Options

A.

Α.Β.Γ.Δ.Ε.Ζ.Η.Θ.Ι.Κ.Λ.Μ.Ν.Ξ.Ο.Π.Ρ.Σ.Τ.Υ.Φ.Χ.Ψ.Ω.

Αἰ.Αὐ.Εἰ.Εὐ.Οἰ.Οὐ.   Αἰ.Ηι.Ωι.Υἱ.

ΑΝΘΟΛΟΓΙΑ ΔΙΑΦΟΡΩΝ ΕΠΙΓΡΑΜΜΑΤΩΝ, ΑΡΧΑΙΟΙΣ ΣΥΝ
ΤΕΘΕΙΜΕΝΩΝ ΣΟΦΟΙΣ, ΕΠΙ ΔΙΑΦΟΡΟΙΣ ΥΠΟΘΕΣΕΣΙΝ, ΕΡΜΗ
ΝΕΙΑΣ ΕΧΟΝΤΩΝ ΕΠΙΔΕΙΞΙΝ. ΚΑΙ ΠΡΑΓΜΑΤΩΝ Ἢ ΓΕΝΟΜΕ
ΝΩΝ, Ἢ ΩΣ ΓΕΝΟΜΕΝΩΝ ΑΦΗΓΗΣΙΝ. ΔΙΗΡΗΜΕΝΟΥ ΔΕ ΙΣ Ε
ΠΤΑ ΤΜΗΜΑΤΑ ΤΟΥ ΒΙΒΛΙΟΥ ΚΑΙ ΤΟΥΤΩΝ ΕΙΣ ΚΕΦΑΛΑΙΑ
ΚΑΤΑ ΣΤΟΙΧΕΙΟΝ ΔΙΕΚΤΕΘΕΙΜΕΝΩΝ, ΤΑΔΕ ΠΕΡΙΕΧΕΙ ΤΟ
ΠΡΩΤΟΝ. ΕΙΣ ΑΓΩΝΑΣ. ΕΙΣ ΑΜΠΕΛΟΝ. ΕΙΣ ΑΝΑΘΗΜΑ
ΤΑ. ΕΙΣ ΑΝΑΠΗΡΟΥΣ. ΑΝΔΡΕΙΟΥΣ. ΑΝΤΑΠΟΔΟΣΙΝ. ΑΠΕΙ
ΛΗΝ. ΑΡΕΤΗΝ. ΑΣΕΒΕΙΣ. ΑΣΩΤΟΥΣ. ΑΥΛΗΤΑΣ. ΑΥΤΑΡ
ΚΕΙΑΝ. ΒΙΟΝ ΑΝΘΡΩΠΙΝΟΝ. ΒΡΕΦΗ. ΓΑΜΟΝ. ΓΗΡΑΣ.
ΓΡΑΜΜΑΤΙΚΟΥΣ. ΓΥΝΑΙΚΑΣ. ΔΕΝΔΡΑ. ΔΙΚΑΙΟΣΥΝΗΝ.
ΔΙΚΗΝ. ΔΥΣΤΥΧΙΑΝ. ΕΛΕΟΝ. ΕΛΠΙΔΑΣ. ΕΠΑΙΝΟΥΣ.
ΕΡΩΤΑ. ΕΥΣΕΒΕΙΑΝ. ΕΥΤΥΧΙΑΝ. ΕΥΧΑΡΙΣΤΟΥΣ. ΕΥΧΗΝ
ΕΧΘΡΟΥΣ. ΖΩΑ. ΖΩΗΝ. ΗΧΩ. ΘΑΛΑΣΣΑΝ. ΘΑΝΑΤΟΝ.
ΘΕΟΥΣ. ΙΑΤΡΟΥΣ. ΙΧΘΥΑΣ. ΚΑΛΛΟΣ. ΚΟΛΑΚΑΣ. ΚΡΙ
ΤΑΣ. ΛΟΓΟΓΡΑΦΙΑΝ. ΜΑΙΝΟΜΕΝΟΥΣ. ΜΑΘΗΜΑΤΑ. ΜΕ
ΘΗΝ. ΜΕΤΡΙΟΤΗΤΑ. ΜΙΣΟΣ. ΜΗΤΡΥΙΑΝ. ΝΝΗΜΗΝ.
ΜΥΣΤΗΡΙΟΝ. ΜΕΜΨΙΝ. ΝΑΟΥΣ. ΝΑΥΑΓΙΟΝ. ΝΑΥΤΙ
ΛΙΑΝ. ΝΗΑΣ. ΝΗΣΟΥΣ. ΟΙΝΟΝ. ΟΡΝΙΣ. ΠΑΙΔΙΑΝ.
ΠΑΝΟΥΡΓΟΥΣ. ΠΑΡΑΜΥΘΙΑΝ. ΠΑΤΡΙΔΑ. ΠΗΓΗΝ. ΠΛΟΥ
ΤΟΥΝΤΑΣ. ΠΟΙΗΤΑΣ. ΠΟΙΜΕΝΑΣ. ΠΟΛΕΜΟΝ. ΠΟΛΕΙΣ.
ΠΟΝΗΡΟΥΣ. ΠΟΡΝΑΣ. ΠΟΤΑΜΟΥΣ. ΠΤΩΧΟΥΣ. ΣΙΩΠΗΝ.
ΣΟΦΙΑΝ. ΣΥΓΚΡΙΣΙΝ. ΣΩΦΡΟΣΥΝΗΝ. ΤΙΜΗΝ. ΤΥΧΗΝ.
ΥΠΕΡΟΨΙΑΝ. ΦΗΜΗΝ. ΦΙΛΑΡΓΥΡΟΥΣ. ΦΙΛΙΑΝ. ΦΙΛΟΣΟΦΟΥΣ
ΦΙΛΟΣΤΟΡΓΙΑΝ. ΦΡΟΝΗΣΙΝ. ΦΡΟΝΤΙΔΑΣ. ΧΡΟΝΟΝ. ΩΡΑΣ.

B.

IMPRESSVM FLORENTIAE PER LAVRENTIVM FRANCISCI
DI ALOPA VENETVM. III. IDVS AVGVSTI. M. CCCC
LXXXXIIII.

EXAMPLE 2: First page of text **B.** Colophon

4

EXAMPLE 2

CATALOG RECORD

ref. no.

	130 0	Greek anthology.
1,2,3	245 10	Anthologia diaphorōn epigrammatōn / $c archaiois syntetheimenōn sophois ...
4,5,6,7,8,9	260	Impressum Florentiae : $b Per Laurentium Francisci de Alopa Venetum, $c III. idus
10,11		Augusti [11 Aug.] 1494.
12,13	300	[560] p. ; $c 22 cm. (4to)
14	500	Title taken from opening words of text, leaf A1v, transliterated.
15,16	500	First edition; compiled by Planudes; edited by Janus Lascaris.
17	500	Imprint from colophon.
19	500	At head of first leaf: Greek alphabet and diphthongs.
18	500	Signatures (Greek alphabet): [Alpha]⁸-2[Kappa]⁸ chi⁸.
19	500	Space for initial letter of first word of title left blank by printer; spaces for initials throughout.
20	510 4	GW $c 2048
20	510 4	BM 15th cent., $c VI, p. 666
20	510 4	Hain $c 1145
20	510 4	Goff $c A765
20	510 4	Pellechet $c 802
21	500	Library's copy lacks terminal blank. $5 [INSTITUTION CODE]
21	561	With the bookplate of the Broxburne library on back endpaper; front endpapers with the bookplate of William Charles de Meuron, Earl Fitzwilliam, and a modern bookplate "pro viribus summis contendo, ex libris A.E." $5 [INSTITUTION CODE]
21	500	Bound by P. Bozerain le jeune in black straight grain morocco, gilt flower and leaf borders and spine, edges gilt; spine skilfully repaired. $5 [INSTITUTION CODE]
	700 1	Laurentius, Venetus, $e printer.
	700 1	Lascaris, Janus, $d 1445?-1535, $e ed.
	700 1	Planudes, Maximus, $d ca. 1260-ca. 1310, $e comp.
22	700 1	Bozerain, $c le jeune, $e binder. $5 [INSTITUTION CODE]
	752	Italy $d Florence

PRINCIPAL *DCRB* RULES ILLUSTRATED

ref. no.

1	0G	(missing guide letter supplied in transcription)
2	1B5	(title taken from opening words of text)
3	1G12	(statement of responsibility without explicitly named person or body)
4	4A2	(imprint from colophon)
5	4B1	(place of publication transcribed as it appears)
6	4B2	(words or phrases associated with place name transcribed)
7	4C1	(printer named in publisher statement)
8	4C2	(words or phrases preceding publisher statement transcribed)
9	4D1	(day and month in date transcribed)
10	4D2, par. 1	(roman numerals in date transcribed as arabic numerals)
11	4D2, par. 5	(Roman-style date)
12	5B8	(pages not numbered)
13	5D1, par. 3	(format)
14	7C3	(source of title proper note)
15	7C6, par. 1	(authorship note)
16	7C7	(edition and bibliographic history note)
17	7C8	(publication note)
18	7C9	(signatures note; gatherings signed with unavailable characters)
19	7C10	(physical description note)
20	7C14	(references to published descriptions; required for incunabula)
21	7C18	(copy-specific note) See Introduction regarding Local Note Options
22		See Introduction regarding Local Added Entry Options

A.

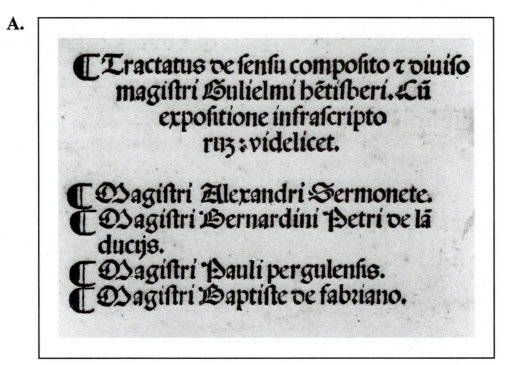

¶Tractatus ꝟe senſu compoſito ⁊ ꝟiuiſo
magiſtri Gulielmi hētiſberi.Cū
expoſitione infraſcripto
ruȝ꞉videlicet.

¶Magiſtri Alexandri Sermonete.
¶Magiſtri Bernardini Petri ꝟe lā
ducijs.
¶Magiſtri Pauli pergulenſis.
¶Magiſtri Baptiſte ꝟe fabriano.

B.

¶Impreſſum Uenetijs p̄ Jacobum
Pentium ꝟe Leuco.Anno ꝟomini
M.cccccj.Die.xvij.Julij regnante
Auguſtino Barbadico ſereniſſimo
Uenettarum Principe.

EXAMPLE 3: A. Title page **B.** Colophon to vol. 1, showing usage of i/j and u/v

EXAMPLE 3

CATALOG RECORD

ref. no.

	100 1	Heytesbury, William, $d fl. 1340.
	240 10	De sensu composito et diviso
2,3,4,5	245 10	Tractatus de sensu composito [et] diuiso Magistri Gulielmi He[n]tisberi : $b cu[m] expositione infrascriptoru[m] videlicet, Magistri Alexandri Sermonete, Magistri Bernardini Petri de La[n]ducijs, Magistri Pauli Pergulensis, Magistri Baptiste de Fabriano.
22,23	246 3	Tractatus de sensu composito et diviso Magistri Gulielmi Hentisberi
22,24	246 30	De sensu composito et diviso
1,2,6,7,8,9, 10,11,12,13	260	Impressum Venetijs : $b P[er] Iacobum Pentium de Leuco, $c anno Domini 1501 die xvij. Iulij.
14,15,16	300	23, [1], 24, 18 leaves ; $c 21 cm. (4to)
17	500	Each part has separate colophon, some with printer's device.
17	500	Imprint from colophon to pt. 1.
17	500	Colophons have dates: pt. 1, Die xvij. Iulij, 1501; pt. 2, Die xx. Nouembris, 1500; pt. 3, Die iij. Decembris, 1500.
18	500	Signatures: A-C⁸, ²A-C⁸ a⁸ b¹⁰.
19	500	Black letter type; text printed in double columns.
20	510 4	BM STC Italian, $c p. 322
21	500	With: Pergola, Paolo della, d. 1455. [Compendium logicae] Logica Magistri Pauli Pergulensis. Impressum Venetijs : Per Io. Baptistam Sessa, anno salutis 1501 vltimo Kal's Decembris [1 Dec.] $5 [INSTITUTION CODE]
	700 1	Sermoneta, Alexander.
	700 1	Landucius, Bernardinus Petrus.
	700 1	Pergola, Paolo della, $d d. 1455.
	700 1	Fabriano, Baptista de.
	752	Italy $d Venice

PRINCIPAL *DCRB* RULES ILLUSTRATED

ref. no.

1	0H, par. 5	(gothic capitals J and U treated as I and V)
2	0J2	(contractions and abbreviations expanded to full form, with brackets)
3	1B1	(statement of responsibility inseparably linked to title proper)
4	1D5	(other title information with inseparable statements of responsibility)
5	1G7	(titles of address in statements of responsibility)
6	4A2	(imprint from colophon)
7	4B1	(place of publication transcribed as it appears)
8	4B2	(words or phrases associated with place name transcribed)
9	4C1	(printer named in publisher statement)
10	4C2	(words or phrases preceding publisher transcribed)
11	4D1	(day, month, words and phrase in date transcribed)
12	4D2, par. 1	(roman numerals in date transcribed as arabic numerals)
13	4D8	(additional dates given in note)
14	5B1, par. 1	(leaves printed on both sides, numbered on one side)
15	5B3	(foliation sequence includes unnumbered leaves)
16	5D1, par. 3	(format)
17	7C8	(publication note)
18	7C9	(signatures note)
19	7C10	(physical description note)
20	7C14	(references to published descriptions)
21	7C19	(copy-specific "with:" note) See Introduction regarding Local Note Options
22	App. A.0H	(added entry for title proper in modern orthography)
23	App. A.0J2	(added entry for title proper with unbracketed expansion of contractions)
24	App. A.1B1	(added entry for chief title)

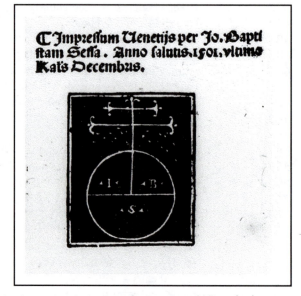

EXAMPLE 4: A. Title page **B.** Colophon to vol. 1, showing usage of i/j and u/v

EXAMPLE 4

CATALOG RECORD

ref. no.

	100 1	Pergola, Paolo della, $d d. 1455.
	240 10	Compendium logicae
2,3	245 10	Logica Magistri Pauli Pergulensis.
1,4,5,6,7,8, 9,10	260	Impressum Venetijs : $b Per Io. Baptistam Sessa, $c anno salutis 1501 vltimo Kal's Decembris [1 Dec.]
11,12,13	300	[72] p. ; $b ill. (woodcuts) ; $c 21 cm. (4to)
14	500	Imprint from colophon.
15	500	Signatures: a-i⁴.
16	500	Printer's devices on t.p. and colophon; initials.
16	500	Text in black letter type.
17	510 4	EDIT 16 $c B704
18	500	With: Heytesbury, William, fl. 1340. [De sensu composito et diviso] Tractatus de sensu composito [et] diuiso Magistri Gulielmi He[n]tisberi ... Impressum Venetijs : P[er] Iacobum Pentium de Leuco, anno Domini 1501 die .xvij. Iulij. $5 [INSTITUTION CODE]
	752	Italy $d Venice

PRINCIPAL *DCRB* RULES ILLUSTRATED

ref. no.

1	0H, par. 5	(gothic capitals J and U treated as I and V)
2	1B1	(statement of responsibility inseparably linked to title proper)
3	1G7	(title of address in statement of responsibility)
4	4A2	(imprint from colophon)
5	4B1	(place of publication transcribed as it appears)
6	4B2	(words or phrases associated with place name transcribed)
7	4C1	(printer named in publisher statement)
8	4C2	(words or phrases preceding publisher statement transcribed)
9	4D1	(day, month, words and phrases in date transcribed)
10	4D2, par. 5	(Roman-style date)
11	5B8	(pages not numbered)
12	5C1	(illustrations; **option:** describe graphic process or technique)
13	5D1, par. 3	(format)
14	7C8	(publication note)
15	7C9	(signatures note)
16	7C10	(physical description note)
17	7C14	(references to published descriptions)
18	7C19	(copy-specific "with:" note) See Introduction regarding Local Note Options

Or
tho
gra
phia
Clarissimi
Oratoris
Ga
spa
rini
Ber
go
mensis

De uerbis quibus frequentior usus est
ꝗ in quibus sepius a recta scribēdi via
deceditur:ꝗ tam de compositis q̄z sim/
plicibus penes ordinem litterarum:ne
quis in querédo falli possit:ac de diph/
tongis ꝗ ratione punctandi.

Collegij Alexand; Bujr. Carp.

EXAMPLE 5: Title page

EXAMPLE 5

CATALOG RECORD

ref. no.

	100 1	Barzizza, Gasparino, $d ca. 1360-1431.
	240 10	Orthographia
2,3,4	245 10	Orthographia clarissimi oratoris Gasparini Bergomensis : $b de uerbis quibus frequentior usus est [et] in quibus sepius a recta scribe[n]di via deceditur ...
1,5,6,7,8,9	260	[Venice : $b s.n., $c 151-?]
10,11	300	[160] p. ; $c 22 cm. (4to)
12	500	Signatures: a^8 b-t^4.
13	500	Woodcut initials (used by de Luere, Venice, 1511, 1514).
14	510 4	Index Aureliensis, $c 114.329
14	510 4	EDIT 16, $c B704
15	500	From the library of Paez, with signature. $5 [INSTITUTION CODE]
	655 7	Autographs (Provenance) $2 rbprov $5 [INSTITUTION CODE]
16	700 1	Paez, $e former owner. $5 [INSTITUTION CODE]
	752	Italy $d Venice

PRINCIPAL *DCRB* RULES ILLUSTRATED

ref. no.

1	0E, par. 9	(interpolations)
2	0J2	(contractions and abbreviations expanded to full form, with brackets)
3	1B1	(statement of responsibility inseparably linked to title proper)
4	1B7	(lengthy title abridged)
5	4A2	(elements of publication, etc. area supplied from several reference sources)
6	4B1	(place of publication supplied in English form)
7	4B10	(place of publication supplied from reference source)
8	4C9	(publisher unknown)
9	4D6	(date uncertain; "probable decade" pattern used)
10	5B8	(pages not numbered)
11	5D1, par. 3	(format)
12	7C9	(signatures note)
13	7C10	(physical description note)
14	7C14	(references to published descriptions)
15	7C18	(copy-specific note) See Introduction regarding Local Note Options
16		See Introduction regarding Local Added Entry Options

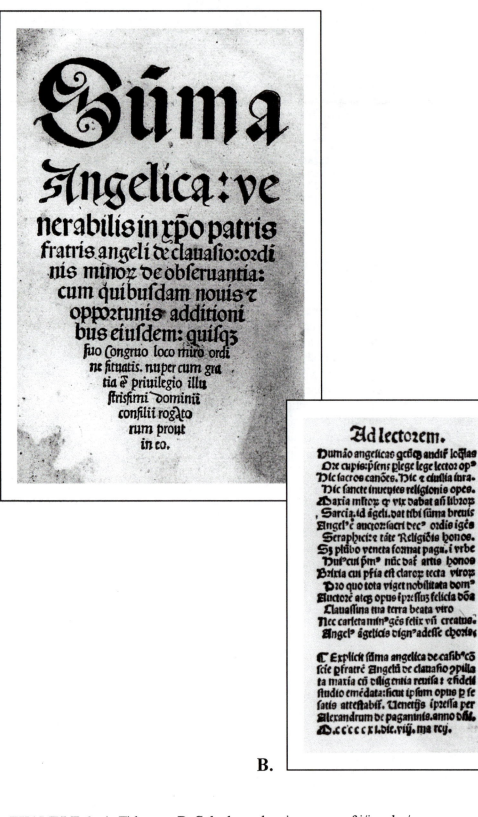

A.

B.

EXAMPLE 6: **A.** Title page **B.** Colophon, showing usage of i/j and u/v

EXAMPLE 6

CATALOG RECORD

ref. no.

	100	0	Angelo Carletti, $d 1411-1495.
1,2,4,5,6,7	245	10	Su[m]ma angelica venerabilis in [Christo] Patris Fratris Angeli de Clauasio Ordinis Mino[rum] de Obseruantia : $b cum quibusdam nouis [et] opportunis additionibus eiusdem, quisq[ue] suo congruo loco miro ordine situatis.
19,20	246	3	Summa angelica venerabilis in Christo Patris Fratris Angeli de Clavasio Ordinis Minorum de Observantia
21	246	3	Suma angelica venerabilis in xpo Patris Fratris Angeli de Clauasio Ordinis Mino. de Obseruantia
1,2,3,4,8,9, 10,11,12,13	260		Venetiis : $b I[m]pressa per Alexandrum de Paganinis, $c anno D[omi]ni 1511, die viij. Marcij.
14	300		[18], 458 leaves ; $c 19 cm. (8vo)
15	500		Imprint from colophon.
16	500		Signatures: pi^8 a^{10}, ^{2}a^{16} b-z^{16} [et]^{16} [con]^{16} [rum]^{16} A-B^{16} C^{10}.
17	500		Text in double columns, 48 lines to a full column.
17	500		Title in red.
18	500		Library's copy in old calf-backed oak boards, with clasp; annotated throughout in an old hand. $5 [INSTITUTION CODE]
	655	7	Annotations (Provenance) $2 rbprov $5 [INSTITUTION CODE]
	655	7	Wooden boards (Binding) $2 rbbin $5 [INSTITUTION CODE]
	752		Italy $d Venice

PRINCIPAL *DCRB* RULES ILLUSTRATED

ref. no.

1	0H, par. 2	(transcribe letters, including i/j and u/v, as they appear)
2	0H, par. 3	(convert to uppercase or lowercase according to AACR2)
3	0H, par. 5	(gothic capitals J and U treated as I and V)
4	0J2	(contractions and abbreviations expanded to full form)
5	1A2, par. 3	(privilege statement omitted without using mark of omission)
6	1B1	(statement of responsibility inseparably linked to title proper)
7	1D2, par. 1	(other titles or phrases following title proper treated as other title information)
8	4A2	(imprint from colophon)
9	4B1	(place of publication transcribed as it appears)
10	4C1	(printer named in publisher statement)
11	4C2	(words or phrases preceding publisher statement transcribed)
12	4D1	(day, month, words and phrase in date transcribed)
13	4D2, par. 1	(roman numerals in date transcribed as arabic numerals)
14	5D1, par. 3	(format)
15	7C8	(publication note)
16	7C9	(signatures note; gatherings signed with unavailable characters)
17	7C10	(physical description note)
18	7C18	(copy-specific note) See Introduction regarding Local Note Options
19	App. A.0H	(added entry for title proper in modern orthography)
20	App. A.0J2	(added entry for title proper with unbracketed expansion of contractions)
21	App. A.0J2	(**option:** added entry for title proper without expansion of contractions)

A. Title page

B. Colophon

C. Running title

EXAMPLE 7: **A.** Title page **B.** Colophon **C.** Running title

EXAMPLE 7

CATALOG RECORD

ref. no.

ref. no.			
	100	1	Erasmus, Desiderius, $d d. 1536.
	240	10	Paraphrasis in Evangelium secundum Joannem
1,2,3,4,5	245	10	D. Erasmi Roterodami Paraphrasis in Euangelium secundum Ioannem : $b ad illustrissimu[m] principem Ferdinandum nunc primum excusa.
19	246	3	Paraphrasis in Euangelium secundum Joannem
18	246	30	D. Erasmi Roterodami Paraphrasis in Evangelium secundum Ioannem
1,4,12,20	246	17	In Euang. Ioan. Paraph. Erasmi Rot.
1,6,7,8,9	260		Basileae : $b In Officina Frobeniana, $c ann. 1523.
10,11	300		[400] p. ; $c 17 cm. (8vo)
1,13	500		Colophon: Basileae in aedibus Ioannis Frobenij, mense Aprili. An. M.D.XXIII.
14	500		Signatures: a-z⁸ A-B⁸.
15	500		Title within historiated metalcut border by Jakob Faber after Holbein. Cf. Hollstein, F.W.H. German engravings, etchings and woodcuts, v. 14A, no. 40.
15	500		Decorative borders; initials; side-notes; printer's device on last leaf.
15	500		Italic type.
16	500		"Illustrissimo Principi, D. Ferdinando ... Erasmus Roterodamus S.D.": p. [3]-[20].
16	500		"Erasmus Rot. Pio Lectori S.D.": p. [395]-[399].
17	500		Bound in contemporary blind-stamped pigskin over boards, clasps lacking. $5 [INSTITUTION CODE]
	655	7	Headlines (Printing) $2 rbpri
	655	7	Printers' devices (Printing) $2 rbpri
	655	7	Borders (Type evidence) $2 rbtyp
	655	7	Pigskin bindings (Binding) $y 16th century. $2 rbbin $5 [INSTITUTION CODE]
	655	7	Blind tooled bindings (Binding) $y 16th century. $2 rbbin $5 [INSTITUTION CODE]
	700	1	Faber, Jakob, $d fl. 1520, $e engraver.
	700	1	Froben, Johann, $d 1460-1527, $e printer.
	700	1	Holbein, Hans, $d 1497-1543, $e ill.
	752		Switzerland $d Basel

PRINCIPAL *DCRB* RULES ILLUSTRATED

ref. no.

1	0H, par. 3	(convert to uppercase or lowercase according to AACR2; transcribe i/j and u/v according to pattern in main text)
2	0J2	(contractions and abbreviations expanded to full form, with brackets)
3	1A2, par. 3	(dedication retained as inseparable other title information; privilege statement omitted without using mark of omission)
4	1B1	(statement of responsibility inseparably linked to title proper)
5	1D5	(edition statement treated as inseparable other title information)
6	4B1	(place of publication transcribed as it appears)
7	4C1	(printer named in publisher statement)
8	4D1	(phrase in date transcribed)
9	4D2, par. 1	(roman numerals in date transcribed as arabic numerals)
10	5B8	(pages not numbered)
11	5D1, par. 3	(format)
12	7C4	(variation in title note)
13	7C8	(publication note)
14	7C9	(signatures note)
15	7C10	(physical description note)
16	7C16	(informal contents note)
17	7C18	(copy-specific note) See Introduction regarding Local Note Options
18	App. A.0G	(added entry for title proper in modern orthography)
19	App. A.1B1	(added entry for chief title)
20	App. A.7C4-5	(added entry for title variant)

A.

C·PLINII
SECVNDI NATVRALIS
hiſtoriæ liber ſeptimus, per Gilber=
tum Ducherium ad Hermolai Bar=
bari, & Beati Rhenani caſtigatio=
nes:maximæꝗ ad collationem
Veteris exemplaris Victoria=
norum reſtitutus.

PARISIIS

In clauſo brunello ad inſigne
geminarum cipparum.

1 5 2 7

B.

I   LIBER·VII.

n proſpexiſſet talem ſolem
ſed e curia. Aeſtimandum

Τέλος.

Errata.
Folio. ſ.facie prima lege maximeꝗ. Fol.ij.facie
prima Adhoc lucis rudimento ne feras quidem:
& ſecunda melius fortaſſe.Serpentem morſu non
petit ſerpens.Paulopoſt lege: At Hercule. Fol.iiij
facie.ſ.capitum bibere. Folio.v.facie.ij.melius le
gas.Eoſꝗ Sciopodas vocari, quia.Folio.vij.facie
ſecūda.Editis geminis raram.& paulopoſt in læ=
ua fœminas.

PARISIIS
Apud Prigentium Caluarin.

EXAMPLE 8: A. Title page **B.** Colophon

EXAMPLE 8

CATALOG RECORD

ref. no.

	100 0	Pliny, $c the Elder.
	240 10	Naturalis historia. $n Liber 7
2,3,4,5	245 10	C. Plinii Secundi Naturalis historiae liber septimus / $c per Gilbertum Ducherium ad Hermolai Barbari, & Beati Rhenani castigationes maximaeq[ue] ad collationem veteris exemplaris Victorianorum restitutus.
15	246 30	Naturalis historiae liber septimus
14	246 3	C. Plinii Secvndi Natvralis historiae liber septimus
1,3,5,6,7	260	Parisiis : $b [Apud Prigentium Caluarin] in clauso Brunello ad insigne Geminarum Cipparum, $c 1527.
8,9,10	300	xxxv leaves ; $c 17 cm. (8vo)
11	500	Publisher's name from colophon: Parisiis Apud Prigentium Caluarin.
12	500	Signatures: a-d^8 e^4(-e4).
13	510 4	BN $c CXXXIX, column 94
	700 1	Ducher, Gilbert, $d d. ca. 1538.
	700 1	Barbaro, Ermolao, $d 1454-1493.
	700 1	Rhenanus, Beatus, $d 1485-1547.
	752	France $d Paris

PRINCIPAL *DCRB* RULES ILLUSTRATED

ref. no.

1	0E, par. 9	(interpolations)
2	0H, par. 2	(transcribe Latin ligature as component letters)
3	0H, par. 3	(convert to uppercase or lowercase according to AACR2; transcribe i/j and u/v according to pattern in main text)
4	0J2	(contractions and abbreviations expanded to full form, with brackets)
5	1B1	(statement of responsibility inseparably linked to title proper)
6	4B1	(place of publication transcribed as it appears)
7	4C4	(publisher's address on t.p. in lieu of name; publisher's name supplied from colophon)
8	5B1, par. 1	(leaves printed on both sides, numbered on one side)
9	5B1, par. 2	(leaves numbered in roman numerals, transcribed lowercase as they appear)
10	5D1, par. 3	(format)
11	7C8	(publication note)
12	7C9	(signatures note)
13	7C14	(references to published descriptions)
14	App. A.0H	(added entry for title proper with letters transcribed as they appear)
15	App. A.1B1	(added entry for chief title)

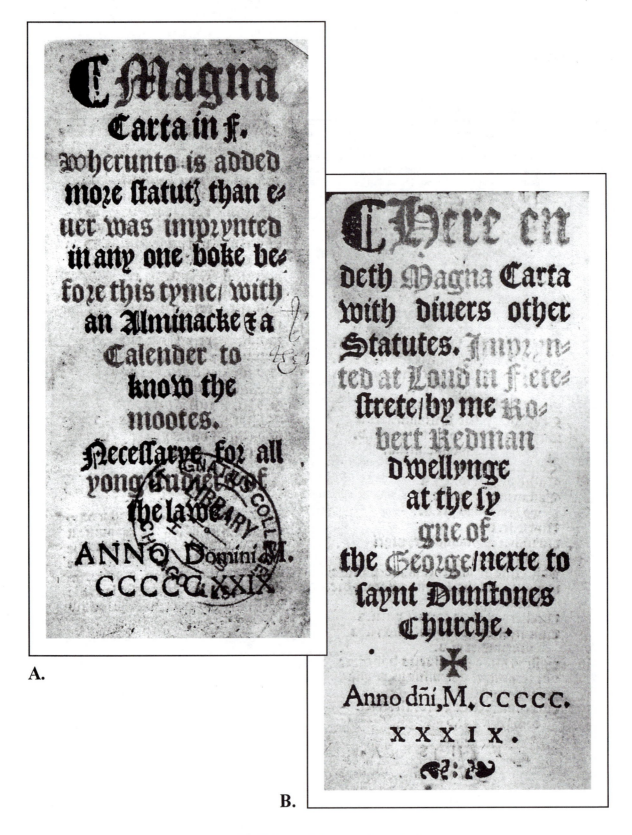

A.

B.

EXAMPLE 9: A. Title page **B.** Colophon

EXAMPLE 9

CATALOG RECORD

ref. no.

	110	1	England.
	240	10	Laws, etc. (Antiqua statuta)
1,2,3	245	10	Magna Carta in F. : $b wherunto is added more statut[es] than euer was imprynted in any one boke before this tyme : with an alminacke [and] a calender to know the mootes : necessarye for all yong studiers of the lawe.
1,2,4,5,6,7, 8,9,10	260		Imprynted at Lond[on] in Fletestrete : $b By me Robert Redman ..., $c anno Domini 1529 [i.e. 1539]
11,12,13	300		[8], 148, [4], 74, [3] leaves ; $c 14 cm. (12mo)
14	500		Contains Magna carta, and statutes passed prior to the reign of Edward III.
15	546		Text in Latin and Law French.
16	500		In two parts; pt. 1, originally published by R. Pynson in 1508, here has the same few additions as Redman's 1525 edition (STC 9269); Redman added the second part in 1532 (STC 9271).
17	500		Place of publication and name of printer from colophon, which gives 1539 as the date of printing.
18	500		Signatures: pi^8 A-T^{12} V^2.
19	500		Title, almanac (leaves pi1v-pi8v) and colophon in red and black; initials.
19	500		Black letter type.
19	500		Errors in foliation: leaves 101, 110-119 numbered 1001, 1010-1019; 108 repeated.
20	510	4	STC (2nd ed.), $c 9273
21	500		Library's copy in old boards; stamps and label of St. Ignatius College; signature on flyleaf of N. Blagdon, and date 1813. $5 [INSTITUTION CODE]
	655	7	Legal works $z England $y 16th century. $2 rbgenr
	655	7	Black letter types (Type evidence) $z England $y 16th century. $2 rbtyp
	700	1	Blagdon, N., $e former owner. $5 [INSTITUTION CODE]
22	710	2	St. Ignatius College (Chicago, Ill.), $e former owner. $5 [INSTITUTION CODE]
	730	02	Magna Carta.
	752		England $d London
	856	7	$u http://www.fordham.edu/halsall/source/mcarta.html $2 http

PRINCIPAL *DCRB* RULES ILLUSTRATED

ref. no.

1	0E, par. 9	(interpolations)
2	0J2	(contractions and abbreviations expanded to full form, with brackets)
3	1D2, par. 1	(other titles or phrases following title proper treated as other title information)
4	4A2	(place of publication and and printer statement from colophon)
5	4B2	(words or phrases associated with place name transcribed)
6	4C1	(printer named in publisher statement)
7	4C2	(words or phrases preceding publisher statement transcribed)
8	4D1	(phrase in date transcribed)
9	4D2, par. 1	(roman numerals in date transcribed as arabic numerals)
10	4D2, par. 4	(incorrect date transcribed as it appears; corrected date added, in brackets)
11	5B1, par. 1	(leaves printed on both sides, numbered on one side)
12	5B3	(foliation sequence includes unnumbered leaves)
13	5D1, par. 3	(format)
14	7C1	(nature, scope or artistic form note)
15	7C2	(language of publication note)
16	7C7	(edition and bibliographic history note)
17	7C8	(publication note)
18	7C9	(signatures note)
19	7C10	(physical description note)
20	7C14	(references to published descriptions)
21	7C18	(copy-specific note) See Introduction regarding Local Note Options
22		See Introduction regarding Local Added Entry Options

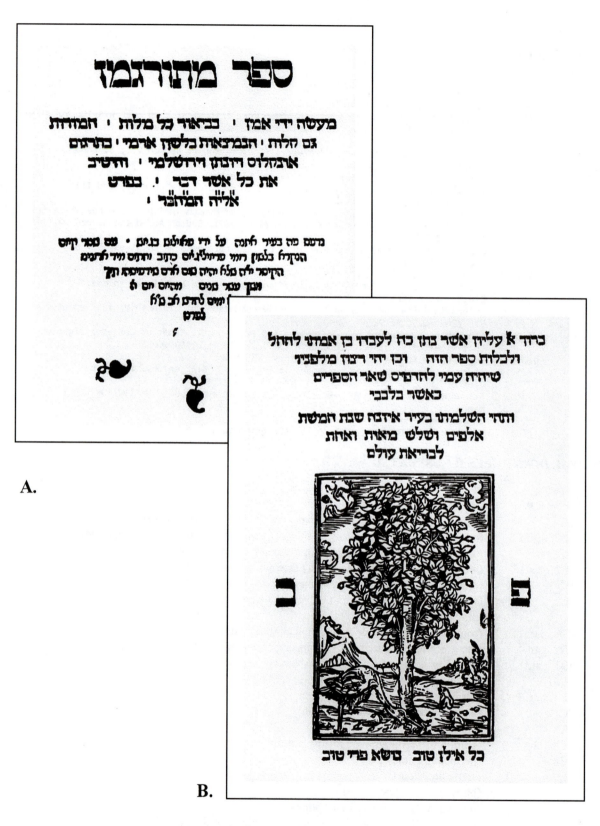

A.

ספר מתורגמן

מעשה ידי אמן · בבאור כל מלות · חמודות
גם חלות · הנמצאות בלשון ארמי · בתרגום
אונקלוס ויונתן ויהושלמי · והשיב
את כל אשר דבר · · בפרש
אלי״ה המחבר ·

מדם פה בעיר איזנה על ידי מלושם בנוב · עם עמר יחס
הנקרא בלשון רומי טרוילנגיוס כתוב ותדפס מידי נאמנם
הקיסר אלה מלא יהיה עם אדם מידטיטאם תקף
מנף עשר ממס   מהיס חם ה׳
יומם להדם חב ם יׄ א
למדם

B.

ברוך א׳ עליון אשר נתן כח לעבדו בן אמתי להחל
ולכלות ספר הזה   וכן יהי רצון מלפניו
שיהיה עמי להדפיס שאר הספרים
כאשר בלבבי

ותהי השלמתו בעיר איזנה שנת חמשת
אלפים ושלש מאות ואחת
לבריאת עולם

כל אילן טוב נושא פרי טוב

EXAMPLE 10: **A.** Title page **B.** Colophon

EXAMPLE 10

CATALOG RECORD

ref. no.

	100	1	Levita, Elijah, $d 1468 or 9-1549.
	240	10	Meturgeman
	245	10	Sefer Meturgeman : $b ma'aśeh yede oman : be-ve'ur kol milot, ḥamurot gam kalot, ha-nimtsa'ot be-lashon arami be-Targum Onkelos ṿe-Yonatan ṿe-Yerushalmi / $c ṿe-heṭiv et kol asher diber bi-ferat Eliyah ha-meḥaver.
1,2,3,4,5	260		Nidpas poh ba-'ir Iznah [Isny, Germany] : $b 'Al yede Pavilus Vagius ..., $c 77,8 meha-yom yom 1, 21 yamim le-ḥodesh Av 301 [14 Aug. 1541] li-ferat.
8,9,10	300		[4], 164, [2] leaves ; $c 29 cm. (fol.)
11	546		Hebrew and Aramaic.
12	500		Colophon: Barukh E. 'Elyon asher natan koaḥ le-avdo ben amato le-heḥel ule-khalot sefer ha-zeh ve-khen yehi ratson mi-lefanav she-yihyeh 'imi le-hadpis shear ha-sefarim ka-asher be-levavi va-tehi ha-shelemato ba-'ir Iznah shenat ḥamishat alafim ve-shalosh me'ot ve-aḥat li-vri'at 'olam.
10	500		Colophon has printer's device with initials P.V. in Hebrew characters and motto: Kol ilan tov nośe peri tov.
13	500		Signatures: pi^4 1-27^6 28^4.
14	500		Gatherings signed in both Hebrew characters and Arabic numerals.
14	500		Leaves numbered in Hebrew characters.
13 |	561		From the library of the Yeshivat Magen Avraham, with the yeshivah's name and shelfmark stamped in gold on the spine. $5 [INSTITUTION CODE]
15 |	500		Imperfect copy: T.p. lacking, supplied in facsimile. $5 [INSTITUTION CODE]
	655	7	Printers' devices (Printing) $2 rbpri
	655	7	Printers' mottoes (Printing) $2 rbpri
	655	7	Non-Latin characters (Type evidence) $x Hebrew $y 16th century. $2 rbtyp
|	655	7	Shelf marks (Provenance) $2 rbprov $5 [INSTITUTION CODE]
	700	1	Fagius, Paulus, $d 1504-1549, $e printer.
16	710	2	Yeshivat Magen Avraham, $e former owner. $5 [INSTITUTION CODE]
	752		Germany $d Isny

PRINCIPAL *DCRB* RULES ILLUSTRATED

ref. no.

1	4B1	(place of publicaton transcribed as it appears)
2	4B2	(words or phrases associated with place name transcribed)
3	4B3	(modern form of place name added)
4	4C1	(printer named in publisher statement)
5	4C2	(words or phrases preceding publisher statement transcribed)
6	4D1	(day, month, words and phrase in date transcribed)
7	4D2, par. 5	(non-Christian-era date)
8	5B1, par. 1	(leaves printed on both sides, numbered on one side)
9	5B3	(foliation sequence includes unnumbered leaves)
10	5D1, par. 3	(format)
11	7C2	(language of publication note)
12	7C8	(publication note)
13	7C9	(signatures note)
14	7C10	(physical description note)
15	7C18	(copy-specific note) See Introduction regarding Local Note Options
16		See Introduction regarding Local Added Entry Options

A.

LA PRIMA PARTE
DELLE HISTORIE DEL
SVO TEMPO
DI MONS. PAOLO
GIOVIO VESCOVO
DI NOCERA,
Tradotte per M. Lodoui-
co Domenichi.

IN VINEGIA appresso Bartho
M D LIII.

S. BARTO

B.

LA
SECONDA PARTE
DELL'HISTORIE DEL
SVO TEMPO.
DI MONS. PAOLO
GIOVIO VESCOVO
DI NOCERA,
Tradotte per M. Lodoui-
co Domenichi.
CON LA TAVOLA DELLE COSE NO-
TABILI, NOVAMENTE AGGIVNTA.

IN VINEGIA appresso Bartholomeo Cesano.
M D LIIII.

S. BARTOLO

EXAMPLE 11: A. Title page to vol. 1 **B.** Title page to vol. 2

EXAMPLE 11

CATALOG RECORD

ref. no.

	100 1	Giovio, Paolo, $d 1483-1552.
	240 10	Historiae sui temporis. $l Italian
1,2	245 13	La prima[-seconda] parte delle Historie del suo tempo / $c di Mons. Paolo Giouio vescouo di Nocera ; tradotte per M. Lodouico Domenichi.
16	246 3	Prima parte delle Historie del svo tempo
16	246 3	Seconda parte dell'Historie del svo tempo
17	246 30	Historie del suo tempo
15	246 3	Prima parte delle Historie del suo tempo
18	246 3	Seconda parte dell'Historie del suo tempo
1,3,4,5,6,7	260	In Vinegia : $b Appresso Bartholomeo Cesano, $c 1553-1554.
8,9	300	2 v. ; $c 16 cm. (8vo)
11	500	Translation of: Historiae sui temporis.
12	500	Vol. 2 has title: La seconda parte dell'Historie del suo tempo ... ; con la tauola delle cose notabili, nouamente aggiunta.
13	500	Title vignettes (printer's device); initials.
13	500	Vol. 1: 526 [i.e. 534], [2] leaves (the last 2 leaves blank); v. 2: 398, [26] leaves.
13	500	Error in paging: v. 1, leaves 529-534 numbered 521-526.
14	500	Library's copy in old vellum-backed boards; book labels of Louis Thompson Rowe; stamp "S. Bartolo" on t.p. $5 [INSTITUTION CODE]
	655 7	Printers' devices (Printing) $z Italy $y 16th century. $2 rbpri
	655 7	Bookplates (Provenance) $2 rbprov $5 [INSTITUTION CODE]
	655 7	Stamps (Provenance) $2 rbprov $5 [INSTITUTION CODE]
	700 1	Domenichi, Lodovico, $d 1515-1564, $e tr.
	700 1	Cesano, Bartholomeo, $e printer.
19	700 1	Rowe, Louis Thompson, $e former owner. $5 [INSTITUTION CODE]
	752	Italy $d Venice

PRINCIPAL *DCRB* RULES ILLUSTRATED

ref. no.

1	0H, par. 3	(convert to uppercase or lowercase according to AACR2; transcribe i/j and u/v according to pattern in main text)
2	1B4	(final number added where title proper includes volume designations)
3	4B1	(place of publicaton transcribed as it appears)
4	4B2	(words or phrases associated with place name transcribed)
5	4C1	(printer named in publisher statement)
6	4C2	(words or phrases preceding publisher statement transcribed)
7	4D2, par. 1	(roman numerals in date transcribed as arabic numerals)
8	5B16	(publication in more than one physical unit)
9	5B20	(**option:** pagination of individual volumes given in note)
10	5D1, par. 3	(format)
11	7C2	(language of publication note; translation)
12	7C4	(variation in title note)
13	7C10	(physical description note)
14	7C18	(copy-specific note) See Introduction regarding Local Note Options
15	App. A.0G	(added entry for title proper without material added in brackets [in the spirit of this rule])
16	App. A.0H	(added entry for title proper/other title transcribed with letters as they appear)
17	App. A.1B1	(added entry for chief title)
18	App. A.7C4-5	(added entry for other title)
19		See Introduction regarding Local Added Entry Options

LAVRENTII
VALLÆ ELEGAN-
TIARVM LATINÆ
LINGVAE LI-
BRI SEX.

* * *

EIVSDEM

De Reciprocatione Sui, & Suus, libellus.

Ad veterum denuò codicum fidem
ab Ioanne Ranerio emen-
data omnia.

VIRTVTE DVCE. COMITE FORTVNA.

LVGDVNI,
APVD HAERED. SEB.
GRYPHII.

1561.

EXAMPLE 12: Title page

EXAMPLE 12

CATALOG RECORD

ref. no.

	100 1	Valla, Lorenzo, $d 1406-1457.
	240 10	Elegantiae
1,2,3,4	245 10	Laurentij Vallae Elegantiarum Latinae linguae libri sex ; eiusdem De reciprocatione sui, & suus, libellus ad veterum denuò codicum fidem ab Ioanne Raenerio emendata omnia.
16	246 30	Elegantiarum Latinae linguae libri sex
14	246 3	Lavrentii Vallae Elegantiarvm Latinae libri sex
2,5,6	260	Lugduni : $b Apud haered. Seb. Gryphij, $c 1561.
7,8	300	754, [54] p. ; $c 13 cm. (16mo)
9	500	Signatures: a-z^8 A-2D^8 2E^4.
10	500	Text in italic type.
10	500	Printer's device on t.p., with motto: Virtute duce, comite fortuna.
10	500	Leaves 2E3 and 2E4 blank.
11	510 4	Baudrier, H.L. Bib. lyonnaise, $c VIII, p. 302
11	510 4	Adams $c V184
12	504	Includes bibliographical references and index.
13	500	Imperfect copy: worm holes through p. 643-664 (leaves S2-T4), affecting text. $5 [INSTITUTION CODE]
13	500	Contemporary full vellum binding, gilt-tooled red morocco spine label, all edges gilt. $5 [INSTITUTION CODE]
	655 7	Vellum bindings (Binding) $2 rbbin $5 [INSTITUTION CODE]
	655 7	Gilt edges (Binding) $2 rbbin $5 [INSTITUTION CODE]
	655 7	Printers' devices (Printing) $2 rbpri
	655 7	Printers' mottoes (Printing) $2 rbpri
	655 7	Italic types (Type evidence) $y 16th century. $2 rbtyp
	700 1	Raenerius, Joannes, $d 16th cent.
	700 12	Valla, Lorenzo, $d 1406-1457. $t De reciprocatione sui et suus libellus.
17	740 02	De reciprocatione sui, & suus, libellus.
15,17	740 02	De reciprocatione sui, et suus, libellus.
	752	France $d Lyon

PRINCIPAL *DCRB* RULES ILLUSTRATED

ref. no.

1	0H, par. 2	(transcribe Latin ligature as component letters)
2	0H, par. 3	(convert to uppercase or lowercase according to AACR2; transcribe i/j and u/v according to pattern in main text)
3	1B1	(statement of responsibility inseparably linked to title proper)
4	1E1	(two or more works by one author, without collective title)
5	4B1	(place of publication transcribed as it appears)
6	4C2	(words or phrases preceding publisher statement transcribed)
7	5B3	(pagination sequence includes unnumbered pages)
8	5D1, par. 3	(format)
9	7C9	(signatures note)
10	7C10	(physical description note)
11	7C14	(references to published descriptions)
12	7C16	(informal contents note)
13	7C18	(copy-specific note) See Introduction regarding Local Note Options
14	App. A.0H	(added entry for title proper with letters transcribed as they appear)
15	App. A.0J2	(added entry for title with expansion of contractions)
16	App. A.1B1	(added entry for chief title)
17	App. A.1E1-2	(added entry for title of additional work)

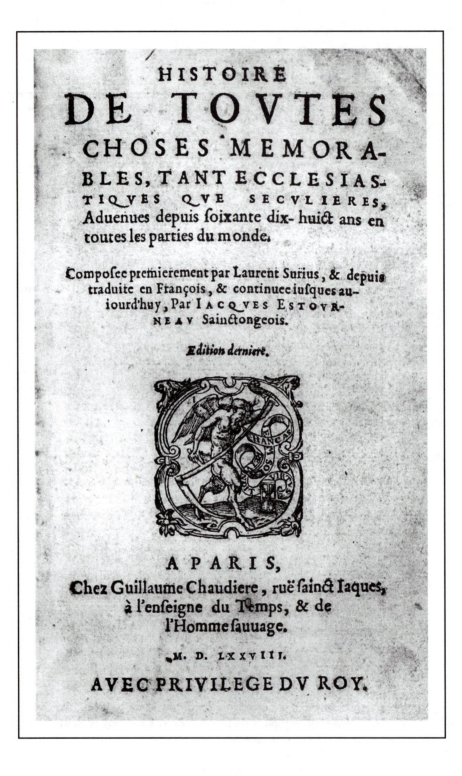

EXAMPLE 13: Title page

EXAMPLE 13

CATALOG RECORD

ref. no.

	100 1	Surius, Laurentius, $d 1522-1578.
	240 10	Commentarius brevis rerum in orbe gestarum ab anno salutis 1500 usque in annum 1568. $l French
1,2	245 10	Histoire de toutes choses memorables, tant ecclesiastiques que seculieres, aduenues depuis soixante dix-huict ans en toutes les parties du monde / $c composee premierement par Laurent Surius ; & depuis traduite en fran.cois, & continuee iusques auiourd'huy, par Iacques Estourneau sainctongeois.
13,14	246 3	Histoire de tovtes choses memorables, tant ecclesiastiqves qve secvlieres, aduenues depuis soixante dix-huict ans en toutes les parties du monde
3	250	Edition derniere.
1,4,5,6	260	A Paris : $b Chez Guillaume Chaudiere ..., $c M.D.LXXVIII. [1578]
7,8	300	[16], 468, [2] leaves ; $c 18 cm. (8vo)
9	500	Revised and updated translation of: Commentarius brevis rerum in orbe gestarum ab anno salutis 1500 usque in annum 1568.
10	500	Signatures: ã⁸ ẽ⁸ a-z⁸ A-2M⁸ 2N⁶.
11	500	Title vignette (publisher's device); initials; head-pieces.
12	500	Library's copy in old limp vellum, with traces of ties; engraved armorial bookplate of Sir William Baird on t.p. verso; marginal notes in an old hand. $5 [INSTITUTION CODE]
	655 7	Printers' devices (Printing) $z France $y 16th century. $2 rbpri
	655 7	Armorial bookplates (Provenance) $z Scotland $y 17th century. $2 rbprov $5 [INSTITUTION CODE]
	655 7	Marginalia (Provenance) $2 rbprov $5 [INSTITUTION CODE]
	700 1	Estourneau, Jacques.
15	700 1	Baird, William, $c Sir, $d b. 1654, $e former owner. $5 [INSTITUTION CODE]
	752	France $d Paris

PRINCIPAL *DCRB* RULES ILLUSTRATED

ref. no.

1	0H, par. 1	(accents not added to "memorables," "ecclesiastique," etc.)
2	0H, par. 3	(convert to uppercase or lowercase according to AACR2; transcribe i/j and u/v according to pattern in main text)
3	2B1	(exact wording if taken from the title page)
4	4B2	(words or phrases associated with place name transcribed)
5	4C2	(words or phrases preceding publisher statement transcribed)
6	4D2, par. 1	**(option:** roman numerals in date transcribed; date in arabic numerals added)
7	5B3	(foliation sequence includes unnumbered leaves)
8	5D1, par. 3	(format)
9	7C2	(translation note)
10	7C9	(signatures note)
11	7C10	(physical description note)
12	7C18	(copy-specific note) See Introduction regarding Local Note Options
13	App. A.0H	(added entry for title proper with letters transcribed as they appear)
14	App. B	(early letter forms)
15		See Introduction regarding Local Added Entry Options

M. TVLLII
CICERONIS
CONSOLATIO, VEL
De luctu minuendo.

Fragmenta eius à Carolo Sigonio,
& Andrea Patritio exposita.

*Antonij Riccoboni iudicium, quo illam
Ciceronis non esse ostendit.*

Caroli Sigonij pro eadem orationes LI.

His admaximè propter argumenti similitudi-
nem, Philisci Græci scriptoris Consolatoriam
M. T. Ciceroni colloquenti præstitam, dum
in Macedonia exsularet, Ioan. Amispa Si-
culo interprete.

VIRTVTE DVCE — COMITE FORTVNA

LVGDVNI,
APVD ANT. GRYPHIVM.
M. D. LXXXIIII.

...per alios excudendos curauimus, lo-
...letes nobis, spero, erunt testes apud
...neis, qui humanioris Musæ sensum
...dò habebūt aliquem, tum noua hęc,
...m te auspice & auctore, vir clarissi-
..., primi nostratium damus. Tullianæ
...solationis editio id testabitur: quam,
...ianæ postremæ (ea ad manuscri-
...rum fidem longè post omneis alias
...igatissima nobis sub prælo est) προδι-
...sub tuo nomine nunc emittimus. In
cuius enim apparere potiùs debeat, aut
tutiùs possit, quàm cuius illa beneficio
in nostras manus primùm peruenit: qui-
que ea sit illustris nominis apud omneis
auctoritate & gratia, vt commendare sine inuidia nouum opus, bonum aucto-
rem, simul visum, simul appetitum, pa-
trocinio suo tueri valeat? Vix intimo
enim Adriatici emersus sinu, longis &
difficilibus itineribus Alpes transmise-
rat; domi tuæ, tāquam in communi Mu-
sarum metato hospitio, cùm ei statim,
in publicum te manuducente progresso,
status quæstio à ciuibus nostris moueri
est cœpta: idque variis adeò dissentien-
tium doctorum iudiciis, vt non leuis
nunc nuper rumor, quanquàm is incerto
auctore, iam percrebuerit, non fortuna-

A 3   rum,

B.

EXAMPLE 14: A. Title page **B.** Page of text, showing usage of i/j and u/v

EXAMPLE 14

CATALOG RECORD

ref. no.

	100 1	Cicero, Marcus Tullius.
	240 10	Consolatio
1,2,3,4,5	245 10	M. Tullij Ciceronis Consolatio, vel, De luctu minuendo : $b fragmenta eius à Carolo Sigonio, & Andrea Patritio exposita : Antonij Riccoboni iudicium, quo illam Ciceronis non esse ostendit : Caroli Sigonij pro eadem orationes II : his adiunximus propter argumenti similitudinem, Philisci Graeci scriptoris Consolatoriam M.T. Ciceroni colloquenti praestitam, dum in Macedonia exsularet, Ioan. Aurispa Siculo interprete.
15	246 30	Consolatio, vel, De luctu minuendo
16	246 30	De luctu minuendo
14,17	246 3	M. Tvllij Ciceronis Consolatio, vel, De luctu minuendo
1,6,7,8	260	Lugduni : $b Apud Ant. Gryphium, $c 1584.
9	300	304 p. ; $c 13 cm. (16mo)
10	500	Signatures: A-T^8.
11	500	Publisher's device on t.p., with motto: Virtute duce, comite fortuna.
11	500	Initials; head-pieces.
12	510 4	Baudrier, H.L. Bib. lyonnaise, $c VIII, p. 389-390
13	500	Limp vellum binding, ties lacking. $5 [INSTITUTION CODE]
	655 7	Vellum bindings (Binding) $2 rbbin $5 [INSTITUTION CODE]
	655 7	Limp bindings (Binding) $2 rbbin $5 [INSTITUTION CODE]
	700 1	Gryphius, Antoine, $d d. 1599, $e printer.
	700 1	Sigonio, Carlo, $d 1524?-1584.
	700 1	Nidecki, Andrzey Patrycy, $d 1530-1587.
	700 1	Aurispa, Giovanni, $d ca. 1376-1459.
	752	France $d Lyon

PRINCIPAL *DCRB* RULES ILLUSTRATED

ref. no.

1	0H, par. 3	(convert to uppercase or lowercase according to AACR2; transcribe i/j and u/v according to pattern in main text)
2	1B1	(statement of responsibility inseparably linked to title proper)
3	1B3	(title proper inclusive of alternative title)
4	1D2, par. 1	(other titles or phrases following title proper treated as other title information)
5	1D5	(other title information with inseparable statements of responsibility)
6	4B1	(place of publication transcribed as it appears)
7	4C2	(words or phrases preceding publisher statement transcribed)
8	4D2, par. 1	(roman numerals in date transcribed as arabic numerals)
9	5D1, par. 3	(format)
10	7C9	(signatures note)
11	7C10	(physical description note)
12	7C14	(references to published descriptions)
13	7C18	(copy-specific note) See Introduction regarding Local Note Options
14	App. A.0H	(added entry for title proper transcribed with letters as they appear)
15	App. A.1B1	(added entry for chief title)
16	App. A.1B3	(added entry for alternative title)
17	App. B	(early letter forms)

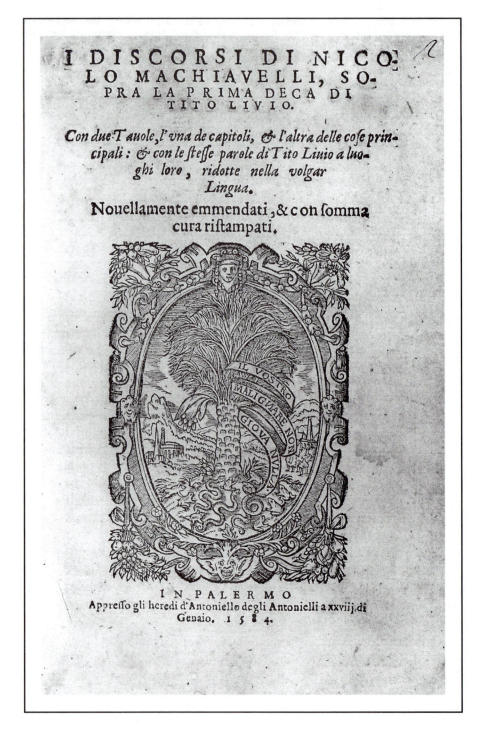

I DISCORSI DI NICO:
LO MACHIAVELLI, SO-
PRA LA PRIMA DECA DI
TITO LIVIO.

Con due Tauole, l'vna de capitoli, & l'altra delle cose prin-
cipali : & con le stesse parole di Tito Liuio a luoghi loro, ridotte nella volgar
Lingua.

Nouellamente emmendati, & con somma
cura ristampati.

IL VOSTRO
MALIGNARE NON
GIOVA NVLLA

IN PALERMO
Appresso gli heredi d'Antoniello degli Antonielli a xxviij.di
Genaio. 1584.

EXAMPLE 15: Title page

30

EXAMPLE 15

CATALOG RECORD

ref. no.		
	100 1	Machiavelli, Niccolò, $d 1469-1527.
2,3,4	245 12	I discorsi di Nicolo Machiauelli, sopra la prima deca di Tito Liuio : $b con due tauole, l'vna de capitoli, & l'altra delle cose principali : & con le stesse parole di Tito Liuio a luoghi loro, ridotte nella volgar lingua.
20,21	246 3	Discorsi di Nicolo Machiavelli, sopra la prima deca di Tito Livio
5	250	Nouellamente emmendati, & con somma cura ristampati.
1,6,7,8,9,10, 11,12,13	260	In Palermo : $b Appresso gli heredi d'Antoniello degli Antonielli, $c a xxviij di genaio 1584 $a [i.e. London : $b John Wolfe, $c 28 Jan. 1585]
14,15	300	[16], 200 leaves ; $c 16 cm. (8vo)
16	500	False place of publication and fictitious publisher; actually printed in London by John Wolfe; the date is old-style. See Woodfield.
17	500	Collation: 8vo: *^{8} A-2C^8 [$4 (-*3, A4; +D5, G5) signed; missigning A1 as B1)]; 216 leaves, ff. [16 unnumbered leaves], 1-80 [81] 82-92 [93] 94-200 (misprinting 48 as 38, 57 as 67, 59 as 69, 61 as 71, 63 as 73, 136 as 135, 171 as 71).
18	500	Title vignette (printer's device; initials).
19	510 4	Woodfield, D.B. Surreptitious printing in England, $c 34
19	510 4	STC (2nd ed.) $c 17159
	655 7	Fictitious imprints (Publishing) $z England $y 16th century. $2 rbpub
	655 7	False imprints (Publishing) $z England $y 16th century. $2 rbpub
	655 7	Printers' devices (Publishing) $z England $y 16th century. $2 rbpub
	752	England $d London
	752	Italy $d Palermo

PRINCIPAL *DCRB* RULES ILLUSTRATED

ref. no.		
1	0E, par. 9	(interpolations)
2	0H, par. 3	(convert to uppercase or lowercase according to AACR2; transcribe i/j and u/v according to pattern in main text)
3	1A1, par. 4	(colon precedes each unit of other title information)
4	1B1	(statement of responsibility inseparably linked to title proper)
5	2B3	(phrase referring to impression treated as edition statement)
6	4A4	(fictitious/incorrect imprint in conventional order, followed by real details)
7	4B1	(place of publication supplied in English form)
8	4B2	(words or phrases associated with place name transcribed)
9	4B9	(false place of publication, corected in brackets)
10	4C2	(words or phrases preceding publisher statement transcribed)
11	4C5	(fictitious publisher, actual publisher given in brackets)
12	4D1	(day, month, words and phrase in date transcribed)
13	4D2, par. 6	(date based on calendar in which year does not begin on January 1; corrected date added)
14	5B3	(foliation sequence includes unnumbered leaves)
15	5D1, par. 3	(format)
16	7C8	(publication note, as required by rules 4B9 and 4C5)
17	7C9	(signatures note; **option:** provide full collation)
18	7C10	(physical description note)
19	7C14	(references to published descriptions)
20	App. A.0H	(added entry for title proper in modern orthography)
21	App. B	(early letter forms)

A.

ELIZABETHÆ,

ANGLIAE REGINÆ

HÆRESIN. CALVINIANAM
PROPVGNANTIS, SÆVISSIMVM
in Catholicos sui regni Edictum, quod
in alios quóque Reipublicæ Christianæ Principes, contume-
lias continet indi-
gnissimas.

Promulgatum Londini 29. Nouembris. 1591.

Cum responsione ad singula capita, qua non tantùm sæuitia
& impietas tam iniqui Edicti, sed mendacia quóque,
& fraudes, & imposturæ deteguntur,
& confutantur.

*Per D. Andream Philopatrum presbyterum, ac Theologum
Romanum, ex Anglia olim oriundum.*

Apoc. 17. vers. 6.

*Et vidi mulierem ebriam de sanguine sanctorum & de sangui-
ne Martyrum Iesu.*

LVGDVNI,

APVD IOANNEM DIDIER.

M. D. X C I I.

B.

14   *Responsio ad Edictum*   *Reginæ Angliæ, Sect. 1.*   35
cùm faces bellorum ac seditionum in omnes cir-   calamitas. Elizabetha, quòd Dominum dererelique-
cumquàque prouincias coniecerint, & tandem   ris; quod viam Regiam religionis Christianæ ac
metuant ne flamarum pars aliqua in ipsos fortasse   Catholicæ deserueris: scriptum est enim. *Quis resti.*   *Iob 9.*

EXAMPLE 16: A. Title page **B.** Running title

EXAMPLE 16

CATALOG RECORD

ref. no.

	100 1	Parsons, Robert, $d 1546-1610.
1,2,3,4	245 10	Elizabethae, Angliae reginae haeresin Caluinianam propugnantis, saeuissimum in Catholicos sui regni edictum : $b quod in alios quóque reipublicae Christianae principes, contumelias continet indignissimas : promulgatum Londini 29. Nouembris, 1591 : cum responsione ad singula capita, qua non tantùm saeuitia & impietas tam iniqui edicti, sed mendacia quíque, & fraudes, & imposturae deteguntur, & confutantur / $c per D. Andream Philopatrum ...
10,17	246 17	Responsio ad edictum reginae Angliae
16,19	246 3	Elizabethae, Angliae reginae haeresin Calvinianam propugnantis, saevissimum in Catholicos sui regni edictum
17,19	246 3	Elizabethae, Angliae reginae haeresin Calvinianam propvgnantis, saevissimvm in Catholicos sui regni edictum
2,5,6,7	260	Lugduni : $b Apud Ioannem Didier, $c 1592.
8,9	300	[16], 278, [14] p. ; $c 17 cm. (8vo)
11	500	By Robert Parsons, S.J., writing under the pseudonym Andreas Philopater. See Backer-Sommervogel.
12	500	Signatures: [dagger]⁸ A-S⁸ T².
13	510 4	Backer-Sommervogel $c VI, column 301, no. 13
13	510 4	Baudrier, H.L. Bib. lyonnaise, $c IV, p. 98-99
14	500	Includes index.
15	500	Contemporary limp vellum binding, printed paper label on spine, ties lacking. $5 [INSTITUTION CODE]
	655 7	Chronicles. $2 rbgenr
	655 7	Limp bindings (Binding) $2 rbbin $5 [INSTITUTION CODE]
	655 7	Vellum bindings (Binding) $2 rbbin $5 [INSTITUTION CODE]
	655 7	Printed paper labels (Binding) $2 rbbin $5 [INSTITUTION CODE]
	700 0	Elizabeth $b I, $c Queen of England, $d 1533-1603.
	752	France $d Lyon

PRINCIPAL *DCRB* RULES ILLUSTRATED

ref. no.

1	0H, par. 2	(transcribe Latin ligature as component letters)
2	0H, par. 3	(convert to uppercase or lowercase according to AACR2; transcribe i/j and u/v according to pattern in main text)
3	1A2, par. 3	(Bible verse omitted without using mark of omission)
4	1G8	(qualifications omitted from statement of responsibility)
5	4B1	(place of publication transcribed as it appears)
6	4C2	(words or phrases preceding publisher statement transcribed)
7	4D2, par. 1	(roman numerals in date transcribed as arabic numerals)
8	5B3	(pagination sequence includes unnumbered pages)
9	5D1, par. 3	(format)
10	7C4	(variation in title note)
11	7C6, par. 1	(authorship note; source of attribution included)
12	7C9	(signatures note; gatherings signed with unavailable characters)
13	7C14	(references to published descriptions)
14	7C16	(informal contents note)
15	7C18	(copy-specific note) See Introduction regarding Local Note Options
16	App. A.0H	(added entry for title proper in modern orthography)
17	App. A.0H	(added entry for title proper with letters transcribed as they appear)
18	App. A.7C4-5	(added entry for title variant)
19	App. B	(early letter forms)

A.

B.

EXAMPLE 17: A. Title page **B.** Colophon

EXAMPLE 17

CATALOG RECORD

ref. no.			
	100 1	Amman, Jost, $d 1539-1591.	
1,2,3,4	245 10	Thierbuch : $b sehr künstliche vnd wolgerissene Figuren, von allerley Thieren / $c durch die weitberühmten Iost Amman vnnd Hans Bocksperger ; sampt einer Beschreibung jhrer Art, Natur vnd Eigenschafft, auch kurtzweiliger Historien, so darzu dienstlich ; menniglich zum besten in Reimen gestellt durch den ehrnhafften vnd wolgelehrten Georg Schallern von München ...	
18	246 30	Sehr künstliche vnd wolgerissene Figuren, von allerley Thieren	
1,2,3,5,6,7,8, 9,10	260	Gedruckt zu Franckfort am Mayn : $b Allen Kunstliebhabern zu Ehren vnd sonderm Gefallen in Truck geben vnd verlegt, durch Sigmund Feyerabends Erben, $c im Iar 1592.	
11,12	300	[108] leaves : $b ill. ; $c 17 cm. (4to)	
13	500	Publisher statement precedes place of publication on t.p.	
13	500	Colophon: Gedruckt ... bey Iohan[n] Feyerabend, in Verlegung Sigmund Feyerabends Erben M. D. LXXXXII.	
14	500	Signatures: A-Z^4 a-d^4.	
15	500	Title in red and black; woodcut title vignette and 108 woodcut illustration initials.	
15	500	Leaves printed on one side only.	
16	510 4	BM STC German, 1455-1600, $c p. 783	
16	510 4	VD 16, $c S 2261	
17	500	Library's copy in 19th-century cloth-backed marbled boards; imperfect: lacks leaves G1 and G4; leaf L1 repaired at lower right margin. $5 [INSTITUTION CODE]	
	700 1	Bocksberger, Hans, $d b. 1520.	
	700 1	Schaller, Georg, $d 16th cent.	
	752	Germany $d Frankfurt am Main	

PRINCIPAL *DCRB* RULES ILLUSTRATED

ref. no.		
1	0E, par. 12	(virgule transcribed as comma)
2	0H, par. 3	(convert to uppercase or lowercase according to AACR2; transcribe i/j and u/v according to pattern in main text)
3	0H, par. 5	(gothic capitals J and U treated as I and V)
4	1G14, par. 2	(phrase transcribed after statement of responsibility; punctuated as subsequent statement of responsibility)
5	4B1	(place of publication transcribed as it appears)
6	4B2	(words or phrases associated with place name transcribed)
7	4C1	(Feyerabend identified as both printer and publisher)
8	4C2	(words or phrases preceding publisher statement transcribed)
9	4D1	(phrase in date transcribed)
10	4D2, par. 1	(roman numerals in date transcribed as arabic numerals)
11	5B1, par. 1	(leaves printed on one side only)
12	5D1, par. 3	(format)
13	7C8	(publication note)
14	7C9	(signatures note)
15	7C10	(physical description note)
16	7C14	(references to published descriptions)
17	7C18	(copy-specific note) See Introduction regarding Local Note Options
18	App. A.7C4-5	(added entries for title variants and other titles)

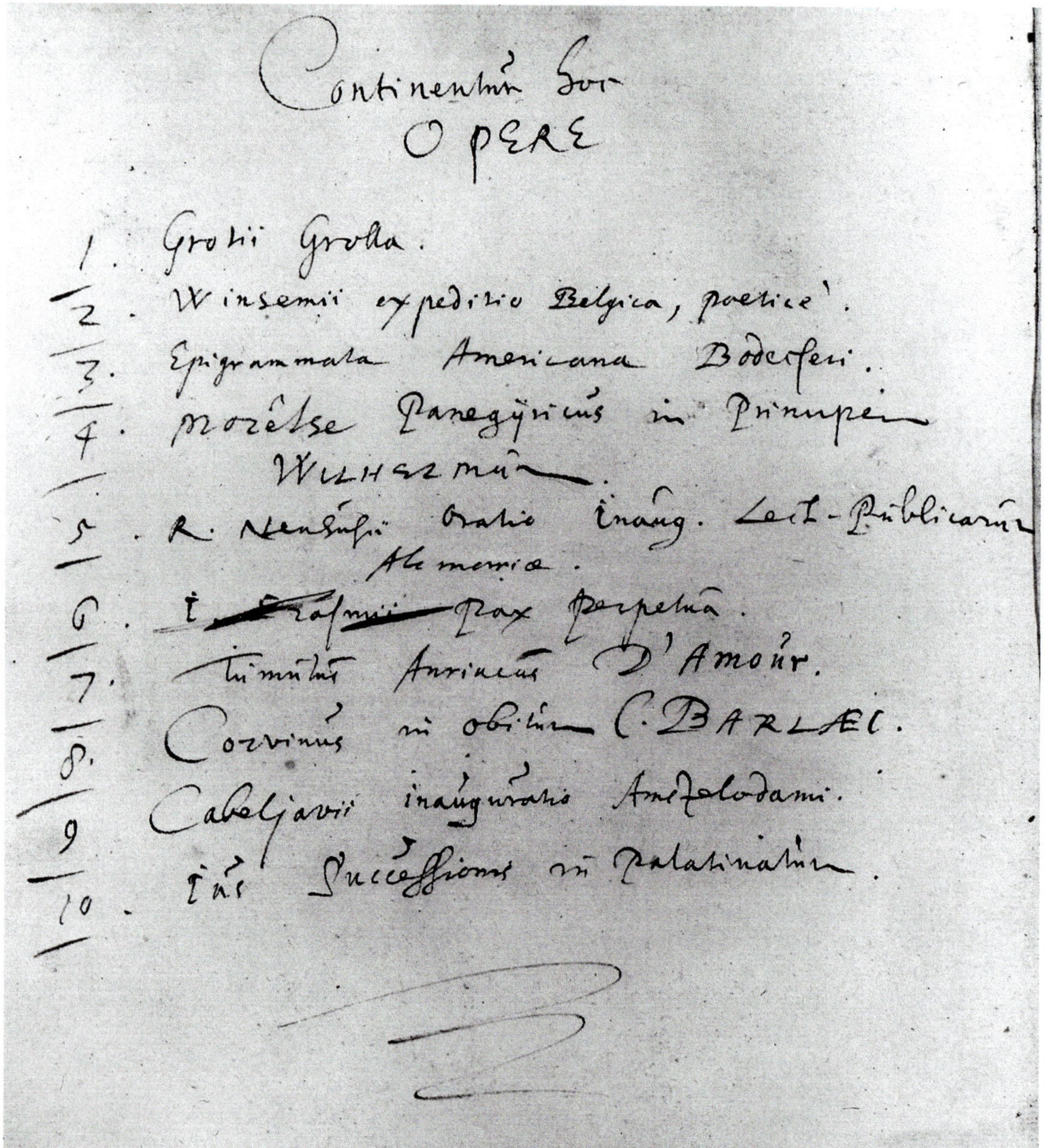
Continentur hoc
OPERE

1. Grotii Grotta.
2. Winsemii expeditio Belgica, poetice.
3. Epigrammata Americana Bodecheri.
4. Morelse Panegyricus in Principem WILHELMUM.
5. R. Neuhusii Oratio inaug. Lect. Publicarum Memoria.
6. I. ~~Erasmii~~ Pax Perpetua.
7. Tumultus Anriacus D'Amour.
8. Corvinus in obitum C. BARLÆI.
9. Cabeljavii inauguratio Amstelodami.
10. Ius Successionis in Palatinatum.

EXAMPLE 18: Manuscript contents leaf of vol. 1

EXAMPLE 18

CATALOG RECORD

ref. no.			
1	245	00	[Pamphlets and printed ephemera concerning the Dutch Wars of Independence]
2	260		$c 1602-1648.
3,4,5	300		ca. 500 pieces in 23 v. : $b ill. ; $c 16-29 cm.
6	500		A collection of pamphlets, broadsides, engravings and other printed material in Latin, Dutch and French, printed at various places in France and the Low Countries between 1602 and 1648; primarily concerning the Dutch Wars of Independence, but also including addresses on a variety of unrelated subjects, funeral orations and miscellaneous official decrees.
7	500		Title devised by cataloger.
8	500		Each volume has manuscript contents leaf in Latin.
8	500		Bound uniformly in contemporary blind tooled vellum.
	655	7	Addresses $z Netherlands $y 17th century. $2 rbgenr
	655	7	Broadsides $z Netherlands $y 17th century. $2 rbgenr
	655	7	Ephemera $z Netherlands $y 17th century. $2 rbgenr
	655	7	Funeral addresses $z Netherlands $y 17th century. $2 rbgenr
	655	7	Proclamations $z Netherlands $y 17th century. $2 rbgenr
	655	7	Blind tooled bindings (Binding) $z Netherlands $y 17th century. $2 rbbin
	655	7	Vellum bindings (Binding) $z Netherlands $y 17th century. $2 rbbin

PRINCIPAL *DCRB* RULES ILLUSTRATED

ref. no.		
1	1B5	(title devised by cataloger from content of work)
2	4A6	(unpublished collection: place and publisher statements omitted from publication area)
3	5B16	(publication in more than one physical unit)
4	5B18	(term "pieces" used in statement of extent to designate items of varying character)
5	5D3	(volumes of a multivolume set vary in size)
6	7C1	(nature, scope or artistic form note)
7	7C3	(source of title proper note)
8	7C10	(physical description note)

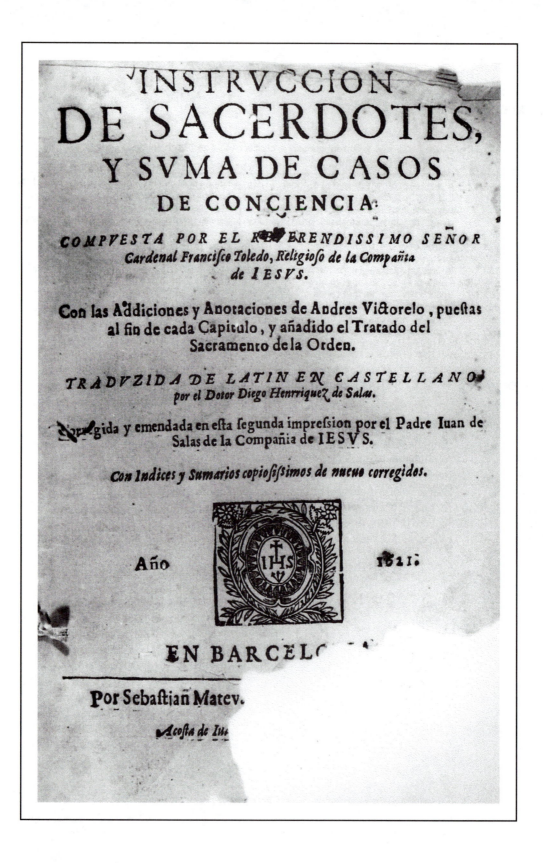

INSTRVCCION DE SACERDOTES, Y SVMA DE CASOS DE CONCIENCIA.

COMPVESTA POR EL REVERENDISSIMO SEÑOR Cardenal Francisco Toledo, Religioso de la Compañia de IESVS.

Con las Addiciones y Anotaciones de Andres Victorelo, puestas al fin de cada Capitulo, y añadido el Tratado del Sacramento de la Orden.

TRADVZIDA DE LATIN EN CASTELLANO por el Dotor Diego Henrriquez de Salas.

Corregida y emendada en esta segunda impression por el Padre Iuan de Salas de la Compañia de IESVS.

Con Indices y Sumarios copiosissimos de nuevo corregidos.

Año 1621.

EN BARCELONA

Por Sebastian Matev.

Acosta de Iua

EXAMPLE 19: Title page

38

EXAMPLE 19

CATALOG RECORD

ref. no.

	100 1	Toledo, Francisco de, $d 1532-1596.
	240 10	De instructione sacerdotum. $l Spanish
3,4,5,6,7	245 10	Instruccion de sacerdotes, y suma de casos de conciencia / $c compuesta por el reuerendissimo señor cardenal Francisco Toledo, religioso de la Compañia de Iesus; con las addiciones y anotaciones de Andres Victorelo, puestas al fin de cada capitulo, y añadido el Tratado del sacramento de la orden ; traduzida de latin en castellano por el dotor Diego Henrriquez de Salas.
25,26	246 3	Instrvccion de sacerdotes, y svma de casos de conciencia
3,4,8,9,10	250	Corregida y emendada en esta segunda impression / $b por el padre Iuan de Salas de la Compañia de Iesus, con indices y sumarios copiosissimos de nueuo corregidos.
1,2,4,11,12, 13,14,15,16	260	En Barcelo[na] : $b Por Sebastian Mateu[...] : $b Acosta de Iu[...], $c año 1621.
17,18,19	300	[8], 1080, [48+] p. ; $c 22 cm. (4to)
24	500	Description based on imperfect copy: lacks lower right portion of title page, and all after p. [48] of 3rd group. $5 [INSTITUTION CODE]
20	500	Translation of: De instructione sacerdotum.
21	500	Signatures: [sec.]⁴ A-3X⁸ 3Y⁴ a-f⁴ (extent of library's copy). $5 [INSTITUTION CODE]
22	500	Title vignette (Jesuit device); initials.
23	500	"Addicion a la suma de Toledo, que trata del sacramento del orden. Por el padre Martin Fornario de la Compañia de Iesus": p. 1053-1080.
	700 12	Fornari, Martino, $d 1547-1612. $t De sacramento ordinis. $l Spanish. $f 1621.
	700 1	Salas, Juan de, $d 1553-1612.
	700 2	Henrriquez de Salas, Diego.
	700 1	Victorelo, Andres.
	752	Spain $d Barcelona

PRINCIPAL *DCRB* RULES ILLUSTRATED

ref. no.

1	0B2	(imperfect copy; no reliable description of missing text available)
2	0E, par. 9	(interpolations)
3	0H, par. 1	(accents not added to "instruccion," "Iesus," etc.)
4	0H, par. 3	(transcribe i/j and u/v according to pattern in main text)
5	1G6	(multiple statements of responsibility)
6	1G7	(title of address in statement of responsibility)
7	1G8	(qualifications retained in statement of responsibility)
8	2B1	(words or phrases associated with edition statement transcribed)
9	2B3	(phrase referring to impression treated as edition statement)
10	2C1	(statement of responsibility relating to edition)
11	4B1	(place of publication transcribed as it appears)
12	4B2	(words or phrases associated with place name transcribed)
13	4C1	(publisher statement includes printer)
14	4C2	(words or phrases preceding publisher statement transcribed)
15	4C6, par. 1	(multiple publisher statements separated by prescribed punctuation)
16	4D1	(phrase in date transcribed)
17	5B3	(pagination sequence includes unnumbered pages)
18	5B12	(incomplete copy; no reliable description of extent available)
19	5D1, par. 3	(format)
20	7C2	(language of publication note; translation)
21	7C9	(signatures note; gatherings signed with unavailable characters)
22	7C10	(physical description note)
23	7C16	(informal contents note)
24	7C18	(note relating to imperfect copy, no reliable description of missing elements available)
25	App. A.0H	(added entry for title proper transcribed with letters as they appear)
26	App. B	(early letter forms)

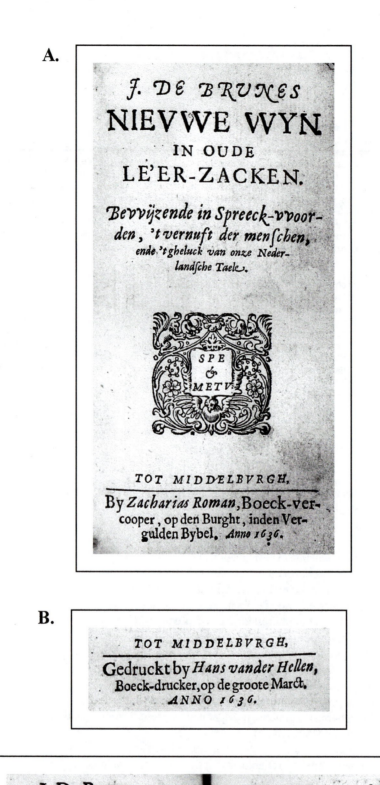

A.

J. DE BRVNES
NIEVWE WYN
IN OUDE
LE'ER-ZACKEN.

Bevvijzende in Spreeck-vvoor-
den, 't vernuft der menschen,
ende 't gheluck van onze Neder-
landsche Taele.

SPE
&
METV

TOT MIDDELBVRGH,
By *Zacharias Roman,* Boeck-ver-
cooper, op den Burght, inden Ver-
gulden Bybel. *Anno 1636.*

B.

TOT MIDDELBVRGH,
Gedruckt by *Hans vander Hellen,*
Boeck-drucker, op de groote Marct.
ANNO 1636.

C.

I. De Brunes	Spreeck-woorden.
n en vanght de wespen niet,	De kraeyen gaetmen licht voor-by
leyne vlieghies, die-ze spier	

EXAMPLE 20: A. Title page **B.** Colophon **C.** Running title

EXAMPLE 20

CATALOG RECORD

ref. no.

	100 1	Brune, Johan de, $d 1588-1658.
	240 10	Nieuwe wyn in oude le'er-zacken
1,2	245 10	I. de Brunes Nieuwe wyn in oude le'er-zacken : $b bevvijzende in spreeck-vvoorden, 't vernuft der menschen, ende 't gheluck van onze nederlandsche taele.
16	246 3	J. de Brunes Nieuwe wyn in oude le'er-zacken
18	246 30	Nieuwe wyn in oude le'er-zacken
10,19	246 17	I. de Brunes Spreeck-woorden
17,20	246 3	I. de Brunes Nievwe wyn in oude le'er-zacken
1,3,4,5,6,7	260	Tot Middelburgh : $b By Zacharias Roman ... : $b Gedruckt by Hans vander Hellen ..., $c anno 1636.
8,9	300	[24], 496, [8] p. ; $c 14 cm. (12mo)
11	500	Printer statement from colophon.
13	500	Signatures: A-Y^{12}.
14	500	Title vignette (publisher's device); initials; tail-pieces.
15	500	Includes index.
17	500	Library's copy in old vellum. $5 [INSTITUTION CODE]
	655 7	Vellum bindings (Binding) $2 rbbin $5 [INSTITUTION CODE]
	752	Netherlands $d Middelburgh

PRINCIPAL *DCRB* RULES ILLUSTRATED

ref. no.

1	0H, par. 3	(convert to uppercase or lowercase according to AACR2; transcribe i/j and u/v according to pattern in main text)
2	1B1	(statement of responsibility inseparably linked to title proper)
3	4B2	(words or phrases associated with place name transcribed)
4	4C1	(publisher statement includes printer)
5	4C2	(words or phrases preceding publisher statements transcribed; addresses omitted)
6	4C6, par. 2	(multiple publisher statements in more than one source)
7	4D1	(phrase in date transcribed)
8	5B3	(pagination sequence includes unnumbered pages)
9	5D1, par. 3	(format)
10	7C4	(variations in title note)
11	7C8	(publication note)
12	7C9	(signatures note)
13	7C10	(physical description note)
14	7C16	(informal contents note)
15	7C18	(copy-specific note) See Introduction regarding Local Note Options
16	App. A.0H	(added entry for title proper in modern orthography)
17	App. A.0H	(added entry for title proper with letters transcribed as they appear)
18	App. A.1B1	(added entry for chief title)
19	App. A.7C4-5	(added entry for title variant)
20	App. B	(early letter forms)

EXAMPLE 21: Title page

EXAMPLE 21

CATALOG RECORD

ref. no.

	100 1	Andreas, Valerius, $d 1588-1655.
	240 10	Bibliotheca Belgica
1,2,3,4,15	245 10	ValerI Andreae DesselI I.C. Bibliotheca Belgica : $b de Belgis vita scriptisq. claris. : praemissa topographica Belgii totius seu Germaniae inferioris descriptione.
13	246 3	Valerii Andreae Desselii I.C. Bibliotheca Belgica
14	246 30	Bibliotheca Belgica
5	250	Editio renovata, & tertiâ parte auctior.
6,7,8	260	Lovanii : $b Typis Iacobi Zegers, $c 1643.
9	300	[16], 110, [22], 900 p. ; $c 20 cm. (4to)
10	500	Signatures: *⁴ 2*⁴ A-O⁴ a⁴ b⁶, ²A-5V⁴ 5X².
11	500	Engravings: title vignette (printer's device); coat of arms on t.p. verso.
11	500	Title in red and black; initials.
12	500	Library's copy in modern calf-backed boards; bookplate of John Webster Spargo. $5 [INSTITUTION CODE]
	655 7	Donors' bookplates (Provenance) $z United States $y 20th century. $2 rbprov $5 [INSTITUTION CODE]
16	700 1	Spargo, John Webster, $d 1896-1956, $e former owner. $5 [INSTITUTION CODE]
	700 1	Zegers, Jacob, $e printer.
	752	Belgium $d Louvain

PRINCIPAL *DCRB* RULES ILLUSTRATED

ref. no.

1	0H, par. 4	(capital I [=ii] not converted to lowercase)
2	0K, par. 1	(initials transcribed without internal spaces)
3	1B1	(statement of responsibility inseparably linked to title proper)
4	1G8	(qualifications retained in statement of responsibility)
5	2B1	(words or phrases associated with edition statement transcribed)
6	4B1	(place of publication transcribed as it appears)
7	4C1	(printer named in publisher statement)
8	4C2	(words or phrases preceding publisher statement transcribed)
9	5D1, par. 3	(format)
10	7C9	(signatures note)
11	7C10	(physical description note)
12	7C18	(copy-specific note) See Introduction regarding Local Note Options
13	App. A.0J2	(added entry for title proper with expansion of contraction)
14	App. A.1B1	(added entry for chief title)
15	App. B	(capital I [=ii] not converted to lowercase)
16		See Introduction regarding Local Added Entry Options

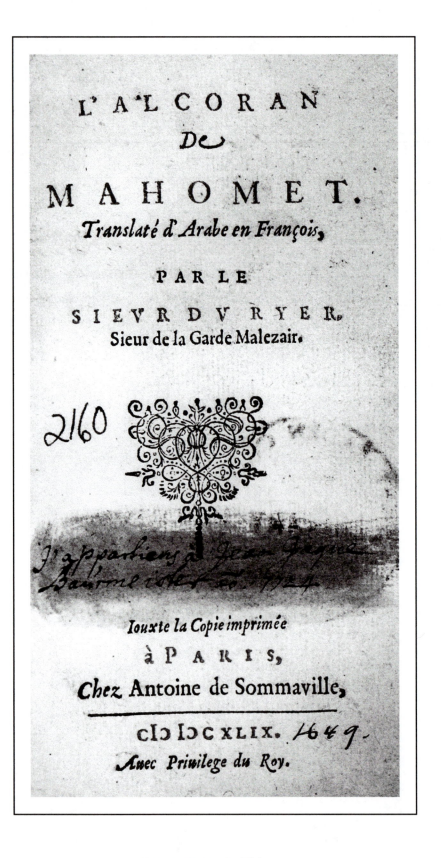

EXAMPLE 22: Title page

EXAMPLE 22

CATALOG RECORD

ref. no.

	130 0	Koran. $l French. $f 1649.
2	245 12	L'Alcoran de Mahomet / $c translaté d'arabe en françois, par le sieur du Ryer, sieur de la Garde Malezair ; iouxte la copie imprimée à Paris, chez Antoine de Sommaville.
1,3,4,5,6,7	260	[Amsterdam : $b Josse Jansson], $c 1649.
8,9	300	[12], 416, [4] p. ; $c 13 cm. (12mo)
10,11	500	Printed in Amsterdam by Josse Jansson; the text is that of the 1647 Paris edition. See Rahir.
12	500	Signatures: *⁶ A-R¹² S⁶.
13	500	Title in red and black.
14	510 4	Rahir, E. Les Elzevier, $c 2019
15	500	Errata: p. [420].
16	500	Library's copy in old vellum; inscription on front flyleaf signed "Jean Josse Schelhofer le jeune," dated 1696; inscription on t.p. dated 1724; stamps of West Baden College. $5 [INSTITUTION CODE]
	700 1	Du Ryer, André, $d ca. 1580-ca. 1660.
17	700 1	Schelhofer, Jean Josse, $e former owner. $5 [INSTITUTION CODE]
17	710 2	West Baden College, $e former owner. $5 [INSTITUTION CODE]
	752	Netherlands $d Amsterdam

PRINCIPAL *DCRB* RULES ILLUSTRATED

ref. no.

1	0E, par. 9	(interpolations)
2	1G14, par. 2	(phrase transcribed after statement of responsibility; punctuated as subsequent statement of responsibility)
3	4B1	(supplied place of publication given in English form)
4	4B10	(place of publication supplied from reference source)
5	4C1	(printer named in publisher statement)
6	4C8	(publisher supplied from reference source)
7	4D2, par. 1	(roman numerals in date transcribed as arabic numerals)
8	5B3	(pagination sequence includes unnumbered pages)
9	5D1, par. 3	(format)
10	7C7	(edition and bibliographic history note)
11	7C8	(publication note)
12	7C9	(signatures note)
13	7C10	(physical description note)
14	7C14	(references to published descriptions)
15	7C16	(informal contents note)
16	7C18	(copy-specific note) See Introduction regarding Local Note Options
17		See Introduction regarding Local Added Entry Options

A.

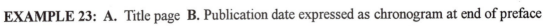

B.

EXAMPLE 23: **A.** Title page **B.** Publication date expressed as chronogram at end of preface

EXAMPLE 23

CATALOG RECORD

ref. no.

	100 1	Schott, Gaspar, $d 1608-1666.
2,3,4,5	245 10	Ioco-seriorum naturae et artis, siue, Magiae naturalis centuriae tres / $c auctore Aspasio Caramuelio ; accessit Diattibe [sic] de prodigiosis crucibus.
20	246 3	Joco-seriorum naturae et artis, sive, Magiae naturalis centuriae tres
21	246 30	Magiae naturalis centuriae tres
1,6,7,8,9	260	[Würzburg : $b s.n., $c 1666]
10,11,12	300	[4], 363, [9] p., 22 leaves of plates (some folded) : $b ill. (engravings) ; $c 22 cm. (4to)
13,14	500	By Gaspar Schott, S.J.; author and probable place of publication from Backer-Sommervogel.
14	500	Imprint date at end of preface, expressed as chronogram: Me ergo frVere aC DIV VaLe.
15	500	Signatures:)(^{2} A-2Y^4 2Z^2 [sec.]^4.
16	500	Engraved t.p.; initials; head- and tail-pieces.
16	500	The phrase "auctore Aspasio Caramuelio" is stamped on the engraved title page.
17	510 4	Backer-Sommervogel, $c VII, column 911, no. 3
18	500	"Athanasij Kircheri Soc. Iesu Diatribe de prodigiosis crucibus ...": p. [307]-363.
19 |	500	Library's copy in old calf, rebacked; imperfect: lacks plate 15. $5 [INSTITUTION CODE]
	655 7	Scientific recreations. $2 rbgenr
	655 7	Chronograms (Publishing) $2 rbpub
	700 12	Kircher, Athanasius, $d 1602-1680. $t Diatribe de prodigiosis crucibus.
22	740 02	Diatribe de prodigiosis crucibus.
	752	Germany $d Würzburg

PRINCIPAL *DCRB* RULES ILLUSTRATED

ref. no.

1	0E, par. 9	(interpolations)
2	0G	(misprint transcribed as it appears)
3	0H, par. 2	(transcribe Latin ligature as component letters)
4	0H, par. 3	(convert to uppercase or lowercase according to AACR2; transcribe i/j and u/v according to pattern in main text)
5	1B3	(title proper inclusive of alternative title)
6	4B1	(place of publication supplied in English form)
7	4B12	(probable place of publication supplied)
8	4C9	(publisher unknown)
9	4D2, par. 2	(date expressed as chronogram)
10	5B9	(leaves of plates)
11	5C1	(illustrations; **option:** describe graphic process or technique)
12	5D1, par. 3	(format)
13	7C6, par. 1	(authorship note)
14	7C8	(publication note)
15	7C9	(signatures note)
16	7C10	(physical description note)
17	7C14	(references to published descriptions)
18	7C16	(informal contents note)
19	7C18	(copy-specific note) See Introduction regarding Local Note Options
20	App. A.0H	(added entry for title proper in modern orthography)
21	App. A.1B3	(added entry for alternative title)
22	App. A.1E1-2	(added entry for title of additional work)

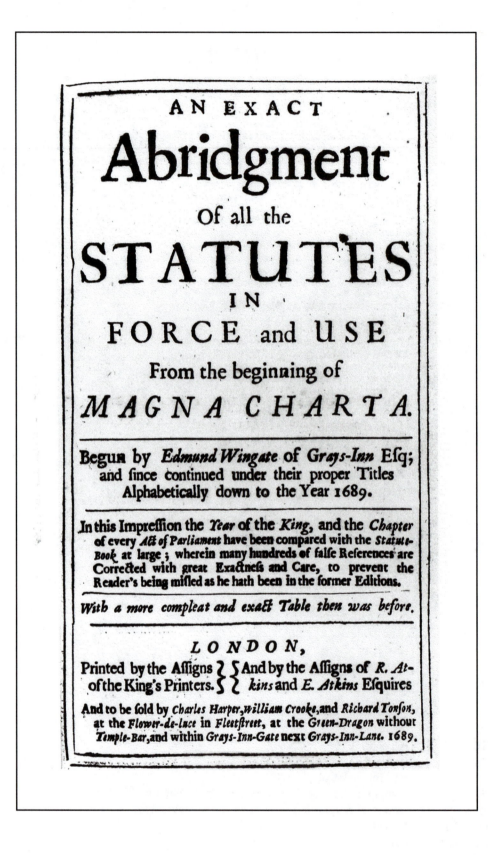

AN EXACT
Abridgment
Of all the
STATUTES
IN
FORCE and USE
From the beginning of
MAGNA CHARTA.

Begun by *Edmund Wingate* of *Grays-Inn* Esq;
and since continued under their proper Titles
Alphabetically down to the Year 1689.

In this Impression the *Year* of the *King*, and the *Chapter*
of every *Act of Parliament* have been compared with the *Statute-Book* at large ; wherein many hundreds of false References are
Corrected with great Exactness and Care, to prevent the
Reader's being misled as he hath been in the former Editions.

With a more compleat and exact Table then was before.

LONDON,

Printed by the Assigns } { And by the Assigns of *R. At-*
of the King's Printers. } { *kins* and *E. Atkins* Esquires

And to be sold by *Charles Harper*, *William Crooke*, and *Richard Tonson*,
at the *Flower-de-luce* in *Fleetstreet*, at the *Green-Dragon* without
Temple-Bar, and within *Grays-Inn-Gate* next *Grays-Inn-Lane.* 1689.

EXAMPLE 24: Title page

EXAMPLE 24

CATALOG RECORD

ref. no.

	100 1	Wingate, Edmund, $d 1596-1656.
1,2	245 13	An exact abridgment of all the statutes in force and use from the beginning of Magna Charta / $c begun by Edmund Wingate ... ; and since continued under their proper titles alphabetically down to the year 1689.
3,4,5	250	In this impression the year of the King, and the chapter of every act of Parliament have been compared with the statute-book at large, wherein many hundreds of false references are corrected with great exactness and care, to prevent the reader's being misled as he hath been in the former editions, with a more compleat and exact table then was before.
6,7,8	260	London : $b Printed by the assigns of the King's printers, and by the assigns of R. Atkins and E. Atkins Esquires, and to be sold by Charles Harper, William Crooke, and Richard Tonson ..., $c 1689.
9,10,11	300	[4], 696 [i.e. 694], [58] p. ; $c 19 cm. (8vo)
12	500	Preface signed: J. Washington.
13	500	Signatures: A^2 B-3B^8.
14	500	Title within double rule.
15	500	Includes index.
16	500	Contemporary blind-tooled full calf binding. $5 [INSTITUTION CODE]
	655 7	Legal works $z England $y 17th century. $2 rbgenr
	655 7	Blind tooled bindings (Binding) $2 rbbin $5 [INSTITUTION CODE]
	655 7	Calf bindings (Binding) $2 rbbin $5 [INSTITUTION CODE]
	700 1	Washington, Joseph, $d d. 1694.
	752	England $d London

PRINCIPAL *DCRB* RULES ILLUSTRATED

ref. no.

1	1G8	(qualifications omitted from statement of responsibility)
2	1G14, par. 2	(phrase transcribed after statement of responsibility; punctuated as subsequent statement of responsibility)
3	2B1	(words or phrases associated with edition statement transcribed)
4	2B3	(phrase referring to impression treated as edition statement; in this case "impression" means "edition" as defined in *DCRB* App. G, Glossary)
5	2C1	(statement of responsibility relating to edition does not name person; prescribed punctuation not used)
6	4C1	(publisher statement includes printers and booksellers)
7	4C2	(words or phrases preceding publisher statement transcribed; addresses omitted)
8	4C6, par. 1	(multiple publishers linked by connecting words; no prescribed punctuation)
9	5B3	(pagination sequence includes unnumbered pages)
10	5B7, par. 2	(error in paging corrected)
11	5D1, par. 3	(format)
12	7C6, par. 2	(other statements of responsibility note)
13	7C9	(signatures note)
14	7C10	(physical description note)
15	7C16	(informal contents note)
16	7C18	(copy-specific note) See Introduction regarding Local Note Options

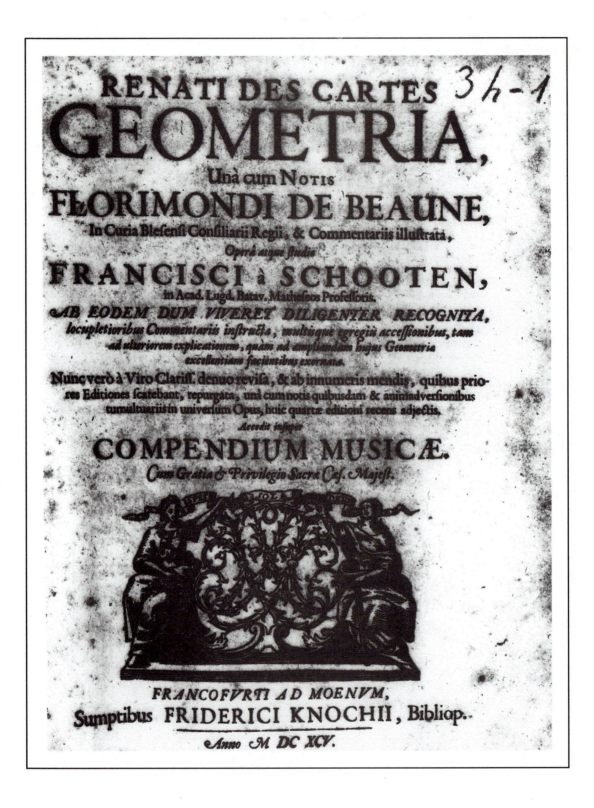

RENATI DES CARTES

GEOMETRIA,

Unà cum Notis

FLORIMONDI DE BEAUNE,

In Curia Blefenfi Confiliarii Regii, & Commentariis illuftratâ,

Operâ atque ftudio

FRANCISCI à SCHOOTEN,

in Acad. Lugd. Batav. Mathefeos Profefloris.

AB EODEM DUM VIVERET DILIGENTER RECOGNITA,

locupletioribus Commentariis inftructâ, multifque egregiis acceffionibus, tam ad ulteriorem explicationem, quàm ad amplificandam hujus Geometriæ excellentiam facientibus exornata.

Nunc verò à Viro Clariff. denuo revifa, & ab innumeris mendis, quibus priores Editiones fcatebant, repurgata, unà cum notis quibusdam & animadverfionibus tumultuariis in univerfum Opus, huic quartæ editioni recens adjectis.

Accedit infuper

COMPENDIUM MUSICÆ.

Cum Gratiâ & Privilegio Sacræ Cæf. Majeft.

FRANCOFVRTI AD MOENVM,

Sumptibus FRIDERICI KNOCHII, Bibliop.

Anno M DC XCV.

EXAMPLE 25: Title page

50

EXAMPLE 25

CATALOG RECORD

ref. no.

	100 1	Descartes, René, $d 1596-1650.
	240 10	Géométrie. $l Latin
1,2,3,4,5,6	245 10	Renati Des Cartes Geometria : $b unà cum notis Florimondi de Beaune, in curia Blesensi consiliarii regii, & commentariis illustrata, operâ atque studio Francisci à Schooten ... : ab eodem dum viveret diligenter recognita, locupletioribus commentariis instructa, multisque egregiis accessionibus, tam ad ulteriorem explicationem, quàm ad ampliandam hujus Geometriae excellentiam facientibus exornata.
18	246 30	Geometria
1,2,7,8,9	250	Nunc verò à viro clariss. denuo revisa, & ab innumeris mendis, quibus priores editiones scatebant, repurgata, unà cum notis quibusdam & animadversionibus tumultuariis in universum opus, huic quartae editioni recens adjectis, accedit insuper Compendium musicae.
10,11,12	260	Francofurti ad Moenum : $b Sumptibus Friderici Knochii, bibliop., $c anno 1695.
13,14	300	[16], 520, 48, [8], 468 p. : $b ill. ; $c 22 cm. (4to)
15	500	Translation of: Géométrie; issued with other works in Latin (not necessarily in translation).
16	500	Signatures: *-2*² 2[star]⁴ A-3T⁴. (Extent of Duke's copy). $5 [INSTITUTION CODE]
17	500	Imperfect copy: all after p. 520 lacking. $5 [INSTITUTION CODE]
17	500	Misbound: p. [3]-[6] bound after p. [7]-[8] (1st group). $5 [INSTITUTION CODE]
	700 1	Beaune, Florimond de, $d 1601-1652.
	700 1	Schooten, Frans van, $d 1615-1660.
	700 12	Descartes, René, $d 1596-1650. $t Musicae compendium.
19	740 02	Compendium musicae.
	740 02	Musicae compendium.
	752	Germany $d Frankfurt am Main

PRINCIPAL *DCRB* RULES ILLUSTRATED

ref. no.

1	0H, par. 2	(transcribe Latin ligature as component letters)
2	0H, par. 3	(convert to uppercase or lowercase according to AACR2; transcribe i/j and u/v according to pattern in main text)
3	1B1	(statement of responsibility inseparably linked to title proper)
4	1D2, par. 1	(other titles or phrases following title proper treated as other title information)
5	1D5	(other title information with inseparable statements of responsibility)
6	1G8	(qualifications omitted from statement of responsibility)
7	2B1	(words or phrases associated with edition statement transcribed)
8	2C1	(statement of responsibility relating to edition does not name person; prescribed punctuation not used)
9	2C3	(phrases about supplementary matter in edition transcribed as part of edition statement proper)
10	4B1	(place of publication transcribed as it appears)
11	4C1	(bookseller named in publisher statement)
12	4D1	(phrase in date transcribed)
13	5B6	(multiple sequences of numbering)
14	5D1, par. 3	(format)
15	7C2	(language of publication note; translation)
16	7C9	(signatures note; gatherings signed with unavailable characters)
17	7C18	(copy-specific note) See Introduction regarding Local Note Options
18	App. A.1B1	(added entry for chief title)
19	App. A.1E1-2	(added entry for title of additional work)

Tyrannick Love;

OR, THE

Royal Martyr.

A

TRAGEDY.

As it is Acted by His Majesty's Servants at the

THEATRE ROYAL.

By *JOHN DRIDEN*, Servant to His Majesty.

Non jam prima peto——neq; vincere certo;
Extremum rediisse pudet.——Virg.

LONDON,

Printed for *Henry Herringman*, and are to be sold by
R. Bently, J. Tonson, F. Saunders, and *T. Bennet*. 1695.

EXAMPLE 26A: Title page

CATALOG RECORD

ref. no.			
	100 1	Dryden, John, $d 1631-1700.
1,2	245 10	Tyrannick love, or, The royal martyr : $b a tragedy : as it is acted by His Majesty's servants at the Theatre Royal / $c by John Dryden, servant to His Majesty.
14	246 30	Tyrannick love
14	246 30	Royal martyr
15	246 1	$i Binder's title: $a Seventeenth-century plays $5 [INSTITUTION CODE]
4,5	260	London : $b Printed for Henry Herringman, and are to be sold by R. Bently, J. Tonson, F. Saunders, and T. Bennet, $c 1695.
6,7,8	300	[10], 58 [i.e. 57], [1] p. ; $c 23 cm. (4to)
3,9	500	Wing calls this the 5th ed.
11	500	Error in paging: no. 55 omitted.
10	500	Signatures: A-H⁴ I².
12	510 4	Wing (2nd ed.) $c D2397
12	510 4	Macdonald, H. Dryden, $c 74e
13	500	No. 2 in a vol. with binder's title: Seventeenth-century plays. $5 [INSTITUTION CODE]
	752	England $d London

The Signatures note reads: Signatures: A-H^4 I^2.

PRINCIPAL *DCRB* RULES ILLUSTRATED

ref. no.		
1	1A1, par. 4	(colon precedes each unit of other title information)
2	1G8, par. 6	(qualification retained in statement of responsibilty as useful for context)
3	2B5	(edition statement from reference given in note; no option to give in edition area. Cf *AACR2* 1.2B4, 2.2B3)
4	4C1	(publisher statement includes booksellers)
5	4C2	(words or phrases preceding publisher statement transcribed)
6	5B3	(pagination sequence includes unnumbered pages)
7	5B7, par. 2	(error in paging corrected)
8	5D1, par. 3	(format)
9	7C7	(edition and bibliographic history note)
10	7C9	(signatures note)
11	7C10	(physical description note)
12	7C14	(references to published descriptions)
13	7C18	(copy-specific note) See Introduction regarding Local Note Options
14	App. A.1B3	(added entry for alternative title)
15	App. A.7C18	(added entry for copy-specific title: binder's title)

Tyrannick Love;

OR, THE

Royal Martyr.

A

TRAGEDY.

As it is Acted by His Majesty's Servants at the

THEATRE ROYAL.

By *JOHN DRYDEN*, Servant to His Majesty.

Non jam prima peto——neq; vincere certo;
Extremum rediisse pudet.—— Virg.

LONDON,

Printed for *Henry Herringman*, and are to be sold by
R. Bently, J. Tonson, F. Saunders, and *T. Bennet*. 1695.

EXAMPLE 26B: Title page

EXAMPLE 26B

CATALOG RECORD USING DOUBLE PUNCTUATION

ref. no.

	100 1	Dryden, John, $d 1631-1700.
1,2,3	245 10	Tyrannick love; or, The royal martyr. : $b A tragedy. : As it is acted by His Majesty's servants at the Theatre Royal. / $c By John Dryden, servant to His Majesty..
15	246 30	Tyrannick love
15	246 30	Royal martyr
16	246 3	$i Binder's title: $a Seventeenth-century plays $5 [INSTITUTION CODE]
5,6	260	London, : $b Printed for Henry Herringman, and are to be sold by R. Bently, J. Tonson, F. Saunders, and T. Bennet., $c 1695..
7,8,9	300	[10], 58 [i.e. 57], [1] p. ; $c 23 cm. (4to)
4,10	500	Wing calls this the 5th ed.
12	500	Error in paging: no. 55 omitted.
11	500	Signatures: A-H^4 I^2.
13	510 4	Wing (2nd ed.) $c D2397
13	510 4	Macdonald, H. Dryden, $c 74e
14	500	No. 2 in a vol. with binder's title: Seventeenth-century plays. $5 [INSTITUTION CODE]
	752	England $d London

PRINCIPAL *DCRB* RULES ILLUSTRATED

ref. no.

1	0E, par. 5	(**option:** original punctuation transcribed with double punctuation)
2	1A1, par. 4	(colon precedes each unit of other title information)
3	1G8, par. 6	(qualification retained in statement of responsibilty as useful for context)
4	2B5	(edition statement from reference given in note; no option to give in edition area. Cf *AACR2* 1.2B4, 2.2B3)
5	4C1	(publisher statement includes booksellers)
6	4C2	(words or phrases preceding publisher statement transcribed)
7	5B3	(pagination sequence includes unnumbered pages)
8	5B7, par. 2	(error in paging corrected)
9	5D1, par. 3	(format)
10	7C7	(edition and bibliographic history note)
11	7C9	(signatures note)
12	7C10	(physical description note)
13	7C14	(references to published descriptions)
14	7C18	(copy-specific note) See Introduction regarding Local Note Options
15	App. A.1B3	(added entry for alternative title)
16	App. A.7C18	(added entry for copy-specific title: binder's title)

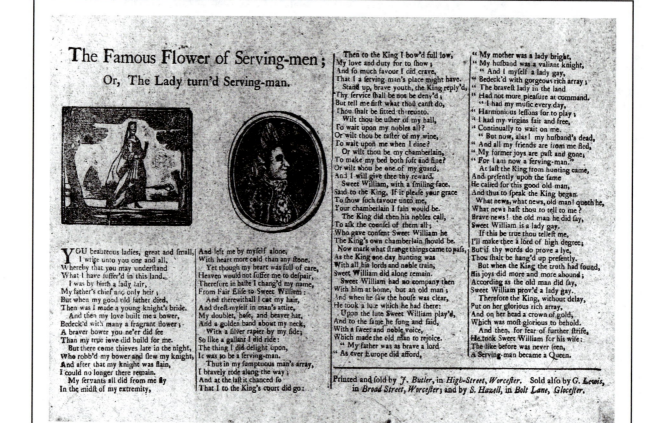

EXAMPLE 27: Single-sheet publication

EXAMPLE 27

CATALOG RECORD

ref. no.		
1,3,4	245 04	The famous flower of serving-men, or, The lady turn'd serving-man.
21	246 30	Lady turn'd serving-man
20	246 3	Famous flower of serving-men, or, The Lady turned serving-man
22	246 3	You beauteous ladies, great and small
2,5,6,7,8, 9,10,11	260	[Worcester, England] : $b Printed and sold by J. Butler, in High-Street, Worcester, sold also by G. Lewis, in Broad Street, Worcester, and by S. Hazell, in Bolt Lane, Glocester, $c [ca. 1705]
12,13,14	300	1 sheet ([1] p.) : $b 2 ill. ; $c 24 x 32 cm.
15,16	500	In verse; begins: You beauteous ladies, great and small.
17	500	An earlier ed. ([1683?] Wing F369A) was signed: L.P. Authorship attributed to Laurence Price by Dr. David Harker in a letter to the Beinecke Library.
18	500	J. Butler was a bookseller in Worcester, 1702-1708. Cf. Plomer, H.R. Dict. of printers and booksellers who were at work in England, Scotland, and Ireland from 1668 to 1725.
19	510 4	ESTC $c n048885
	700 0	L. P. $q (Laurence Price), $d fl. 1625-1680?
	700 1	Butler, John, $d fl. 1702-1708, $e printer.
	700 1	Lewis, G., $e bookseller.
	700 1	Hazell, S., $e bookseller.
	752	England $d Worcester
	752	England $d Gloucester

PRINCIPAL *DCRB* RULES ILLUSTRATED

ref. no.		
1	0D	(prescribed sources of information for single-sheet publication)
2	0E, par. 9	(interpolations)
3	1B3	(title proper inclusive of alternative title)
4	1F2	(begin transcription of single sheet publications with first line of printing)
5	4B8	(place of publication appears only as part of another area; supplied in modern English form)
6	4C1	(publisher statement includes printer and booksellers)
7	4C2	(words or phrases preceding publisher statement transcribed; **option:** address included)
8	4C3	(place of publication transcribed as part of publisher statement)
9	4C6, par. 1	(multiple publishers linked by connecting words; no prescribed punctuation)
10	4D5	(conjectural date based on address of printer)
11	4D6	(date uncertain; "approximate date" pattern used)
12	5B15	(pagination statement for single-sheet publications)
13	5C4	(number of illustrations)
14	5D5	(size of single-sheet publications)
15	7C1	(nature, scope or artistic form note)
16	7C4	(variation in title note)
17	7C6, par. 1	(authorship note; source of attribution included)
18	7C8	(publication note)
19	7C14	(references to published descriptions)
20	App. A.0H	(added entry for title proper in modern orthography)
21	App. A.1B3	(added entry for alternative title)
22	App. A.7C4-5	(added entry for other title)

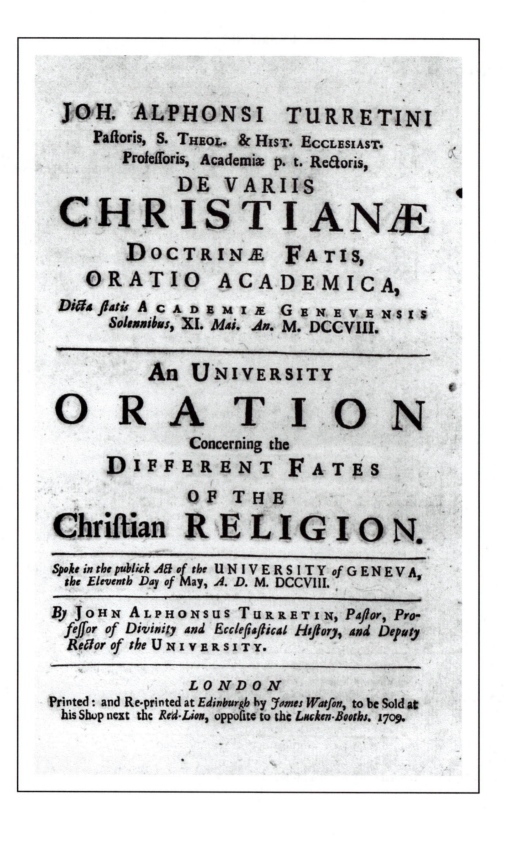

EXAMPLE 28: Title page

EXAMPLE 28

CATALOG RECORD

ref. no.

	100 1	Turrettini, Jean Alphonse, $d 1671-1737.
	240 10	De variis Christianae doctrinae fatis, oratio academica. $l English & Latin
2,3,4,5,6, 7,8,9	245 10	Joh. Alphonsi Turretini pastoris, s. theol. & hist. ecclesiast. professoris ... De variis Christianae doctrinae fatis, oratio academica ... = $b An university oration concerning the different fates of the Christian religion ... / $c by John Alphonsus Turretin ...
18	246 30	De variis Christianae doctrinae fatis, oratio academica
19	246 31	University oration concerning the different fates of the Christian religion
1,3,10,11,12, 13	260	[Edinburgh] : $b London printed and re-printed at Edinburgh by James Watson, to be sold at his shop next the Red-Lion, opposite to the Lucken-Booths, $c 1709.
14,15	300	[4], 35, [1] p. ; $c 24 cm. (4to)
16	500	"Spoke in the publick act of the University of Geneva, the eleventh day of May, A.D. M.DCCVIII."
17	546	Latin and English texts in parallel columns.
	655 7	Addresses. $2 rbgenr
	752	Scotland $d Edinburgh

PRINCIPAL *DCRB* RULES ILLUSTRATED

ref. no.

1	0E, par. 9	(interpolations)
2	0H, par. 2	(transcribe Latin ligature as component letters)
3	0H, par. 3	(convert to uppercase or lowercase according to AACR2; transcribe i/j and u/v according to pattern in main text)
4	1B1	(statement of responsibility inseparably linked to title proper)
5	1B7	(qualifications retained so as not to abridge title proper before sixth word)
6	1B7	(lengthy author statement preceding chief title abridged after sixth word)
7	1C	(parallel title)
8	1D4	(lengthy other title information abridged)
9	1G8	(qualifications omitted from statement of responsibility)
10	4B8	(place of publication appears only as part of another area; supplied in modern English form)
11	4C1	(printer/bookseller named in publisher statement)
12	4C2	(address included in publisher statement)
13	4C3	(place of publication transcribed as part of publisher statement)
14	5B3	(pagination sequence includes unnumbered pages)
15	5D1, par. 3	(format)
16	7C1	(nature, scope or artistic form note)
17	7C2	(language of publication note)
18	App. A.1B1	(added entry for chief title)
19	App. A.7C4-5	(added entry for parallel title)

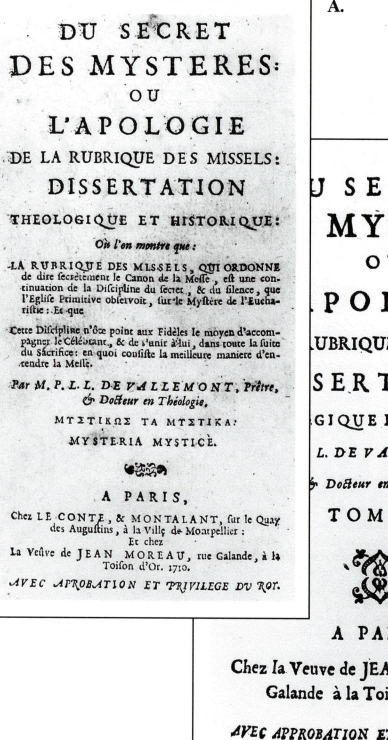

A.

DU SECRET
DES MYSTERES:
OU
L'APOLOGIE
DE LA RUBRIQUE DES MISSELS:
DISSERTATION
THEOLOGIQUE ET HISTORIQUE:

Où l'on montre que:

LA RUBRIQUE DES MISSELS, QUI ORDONNE
de dire secrètement le Canon de la Messe, est une con-
tinuation de la Discipline du secret, & du silence, que
l'Eglise Primitive observoit, sur le Mystère de l'Eucha-
ristie: Et que

Cette Discipline n'ôte point aux Fidèles le moyen d'accom-
pagner le Célébrant, & de s'unir à lui, dans toute la suite
du Sacrifice: en quoi consiste la meilleure maniere d'en-
tendre la Messe.

Par M. P. L. L. DE VALLEMONT, Prêtre,
& Docteur en Théologie,

ΜΥΣΤΙΚΩΣ ΤΑ ΜΥΣΤΙΚΑ:

MYSTERIA MYSTICÈ.

A PARIS,
Chez LE CONTE, & MONTALANT, sur le Quay
des Augustins, à la Ville de Montpellier:
Et chez
La Veûve de JEAN MOREAU, rue Galande, à la
Toison d'Or. 1710.

AVEC APROBATION ET PRIVILEGE DV ROY.

U SECRET
MYSTERES:
OU
POLOGIE
UBRIQUE DES MISSELS:
SERTATION
GIQUE ET HISTORIQUE,
L. DE VALLEMONT, *Prêtre,*
& Docteur en Theologie.

TOME II.

A PARIS,
Chez la Veuve de JEAN MOREAU, ruë
Galande à la Toison d'Or. 1710.

AVEC APPROBATION ET PRIVILEGE DV ROY.

B.

EXAMPLE 29: **A.** Title page to vol. 1 **B.** Title page to vol. 2, showing variant publisher statement

EXAMPLE 29

CATALOG RECORD

ref. no.

	100 1	Vallemont, $c abbé de $q (Pierre Le Lorrain), $d 1649-1721.
1,2,3,4,5,6,7,8	245 10	Du secret des mysteres, ou, L'apologie de la rubrique des missels : $b dissertation theologique et historique ... / $c par M. P.L.L. de Vallemont ...
20	246 10	Apologie de la rubrique des missels
9,10,11,12	260	A Paris : $b Chez Le Conte & Montalant ... et chez la veûve de Jean Moreau ..., $c 1710.
13,14,15	300	2 v. ; $c 18 cm. (8vo)
16	500	A criticism of Vert's Explication simple, littérale et historique des cérémonies de l'Eglise.
17	500	Vol. 2 has variant publisher statement: Chez la veuve de Jean Moreau ...
18	500	Initial; head-pieces (1 engraved) and tail-pieces.
19	500	Imperfect copy: v. 2, p. 297-298 torn, affecting text. $5 [INSTITUTION CODE]
20	500	Bound in 1 v., in full sprinkled calf, gilt-tooled spine, brown leather spine label, red sprinkled edges. $5 [INSTITUTION CODE]
	655 7	Sprinkled calf bindings (Binding) $2 rbbin $5 [INSTITUTION CODE]
	655 7	Sprinkled edges (Binding) $2 rbbin $5 [INSTITUTION CODE]
	752	France $d Paris

PRINCIPAL *DCRB* RULES ILLUSTRATED

ref. no.

1	0H, par. 1	(accents not added to "mysteres" or "theologique")
2	0K, par. 1	(initials transcribed without internal spaces)
3	0K, par. 3	(space between two distinct initialisms)
4	1A2, par. 3	(epigram and privilege statement omitted without using mark of omission)
5	1B3	(title proper inclusive of alternative title)
6	1D4	(lengthy other title information abridged)
7	1G7	(title of address in statement of responsibility)
8	1G8	(qualifications omitted from statement of responsibility)
9	4B2	(words or phrases associated with place name transcribed)
10	4C2	(words or phrases preceding publisher statement transcribed; addresses omitted)
11	4C6, par. 1	(multiple publishers linked by connecting words; no prescribed punctuation)
12	4C7	(publisher statement of v. 1 transcribed)
13	5B16	(publication in more than one physical unit)
14	5B16, par. 3	(issued and bound in different number of volumes)
15	5D1, par. 3	(format)
16	7C1	(nature, scope or artistic form note)
17	7C8	(publication note)
18	7C10	(physical description note)
19	7C18	(copy-specific note) See Introduction regarding Local Note Options
21	App. A.1B3	(added entry for alternative title)

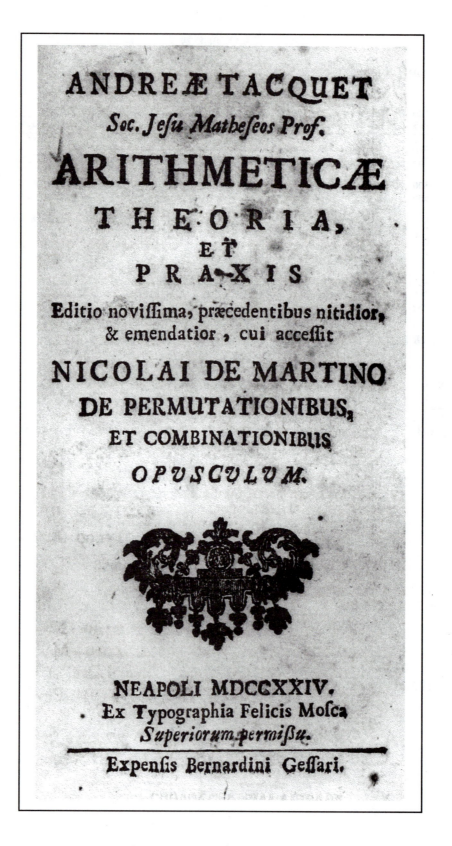

EXAMPLE 30: Title page

EXAMPLE 30

CATALOG RECORD

ref. no.

	100 1	Tacquet, André, $d 1612-1660.
	240 10	Arithmeticae theoria et praxis
1,2,3,4	245 10	Andreae Tacquet Soc. Jesu matheseos prof. Arithmeticae theoria, et praxis.
200	246 30	Arithmeticae theoria et praxis
5,6	250	Editio novissima, praecedentibus nitidior, & emendatior / $b cui accessit Nicolai de Martino De permutationibus, et combinationibus opusculum.
7,8,9	260	Neapoli : $b Ex typographia Felicis Mosca : $b Expensis Bernardini Gessari, $c 1724.
10,11,12,13 14,15	300	[16], 574, [2] p., XII folded leaves of plates : $b ill. (engravings) ; $c 18 cm. (8vo)
16	500	Signatures: a⁸ A-2N⁸.
17	500	Title vignette; initials.
18	510 4	Backer-Sommervogel $c VII, column 1810, no. 6
19	500	"Nicolai de Martino De permutationibus, et combinationibus opusculum": p. [531]-574.
	700 12	Martino, Nicolò di, $d 1701-1769. $t De permutationibus et combinationibus opusculum.
	700 1	Mosca, Felice Carlo, $e printer.
	700 1	Gessari, Bernardino, $e publisher.
21	740 02	De permutationibus et combinationibus opusculum.
	752	Italy $d Naples

PRINCIPAL *DCRB* RULES ILLUSTRATED

ref. no.

1	0H, par. 2	(transcribe Latin ligature as component letters)
2	1B1	(statement of responsibility inseparably linked to title proper)
3	1B7	(qualifications retained so as not to abridge title proper before sixth word)
4	1G8	(qualifications retained in statement of responsibility)
5	2B1	(words or phrases associated with edition statement transcribed)
6	2C3	(edition statement includes statement of responsibility for a work not necessarily appended to other editions)
7	4C1	(publisher statement includes printer)
8	4C2	(words or phrases preceding publisher statement transcribed)
9	4C6, par. 1	(multiple publisher statements separated by prescribed punctuation)
10	5B1, par. 2	(leaves numbered in roman numerals, transcribed uppercase as they appear)
11	5B3	(pagination sequence includes unnumbered pages)
12	5B9	(leaves of plates)
13	5B10	(folded leaves)
14	5C1	(illustrations; **option:** describe graphic process or technique)
15	5D1, par. 3	(format)
16	7C9	(signatures note)
17	7C10	(physical description note)
18	7C14	(references to published descriptions)
19	7C16	(informal contents note)
20	App. A.1B1	(added entry for chief title)
21	App. A.1E1-2	(added entry for title of additional work)

POEMS

ON

Several Occasions.

By Mr. JOHN GAY.

His jocamur, ludimus, amamus, dolemus, que-
rimur, irascimur; describimus aliquid modò
pressius, modò elatius: atque ipsâ varietate
tentamus efficere, ut alia aliis, quædam
fortasse omnibus placeant. Plin. Epist.

DUBLIN:

Printed by S. POWELL,

FOR GEORGE RISK, at *Shakespear's* Head,
GEORGE EWING, at the *Angel* and *Bible*, and
WILLIAM SMITH, at the *Hercules*, Book-
sellers in *Dame's-street*, MDCCXXIX.

EXAMPLE 31: Title page

EXAMPLE 31

CATALOG RECORD

ref. no.

ref. no.			
	100	1	Gay, John, $d 1685-1732.
1,2	245	10	Poems on several occasions / $c by Mr. John Gay.
3,4,5,6	260		Dublin : $b Printed by S. Powell, for George Risk ..., George Ewing ..., and William Smith ..., booksellers ..., $c 1729.
7,8	300		[8], 410, [2] p. ; $c 17 cm. (12mo)
9	500		Signatures: [A]⁴ B-L⁸·⁴ M-Q¹² R-2G⁸·⁴ 2H².
10	500		Head- and tail-pieces; initials.
11	510	4	ESTC $c t013894
12	500		Subscriber's list: p. [3]-[5] (1st group).
13	500		Advertisements: p. [1]-[2] (3rd group).
12	504		Includes bibliographical references and indexes.
14	505	0	Rural sports -- The fan -- The shepherd's week in six pastorals -- Trivia, or, The art of walking the streets of London -- The what d'ye call it -- Epistles on several occasions -- Tales -- Eclogues -- Miscellanies -- Dione -- Fables.
15	500		Half leather, marbled boards, black leather spine label. $5 [INSTITUTION CODE]
15	500		From the library of Eliz. Burroughs, with her signature. $5 [INSTITUTION CODE]
	655	7	Occasional poems. $2 rbgenr
	655	7	Subscription lists (Publishing) $z Ireland $z Dublin $y 1729. $2 rbpub
	655	7	Half bindings (Binding) $2 rbbin $5 [INSTITUTION CODE]
	655	7	Autographs (Provenance) $x Women $y 18th century. $2 rbprov $5 [INSTITUTION CODE]
16	700	1	Burroughs, Eliz., $e former owner. $5 [INSTITUTION CODE]
	752		Ireland $d Dublin

Signatures: $[A]^4$ $B-L^{8.4}$ $M-Q^{12}$ $R-2G^{8.4}$ $2H^2$.

PRINCIPAL *DCRB* RULES ILLUSTRATED

ref. no.

1	1A2, par. 3	(epigram omitted without using mark of omission)
2	1G7	(title of address in statement of responsibility)
3	4C1	(publisher statement includes printer and booksellers)
4	4C2	(words or phrases preceding publisher statement transcribed; addresses omitted)
5	4C6, par. 1	(multiple publishers linked by connecting words; no prescribed punctuation)
6	4D2, par. 1	(roman numerals in date transcribed as arabic numerals)
7	5B3	(pagination sequence includes unnumbered pages)
8	5D1, par. 3	(format)
9	7C9	(signatures note)
10	7C10	(physical description note)
11	7C14	(references to published descriptions)
12	7C16	(informal contents note)
13	7C16	(informal contents note: advertisements)
14	7C16	(formal contents note)
15	7C18	(copy-specific note) See Introduction regarding Local Note Options
16		See Introduction regarding Local Added Entry Options

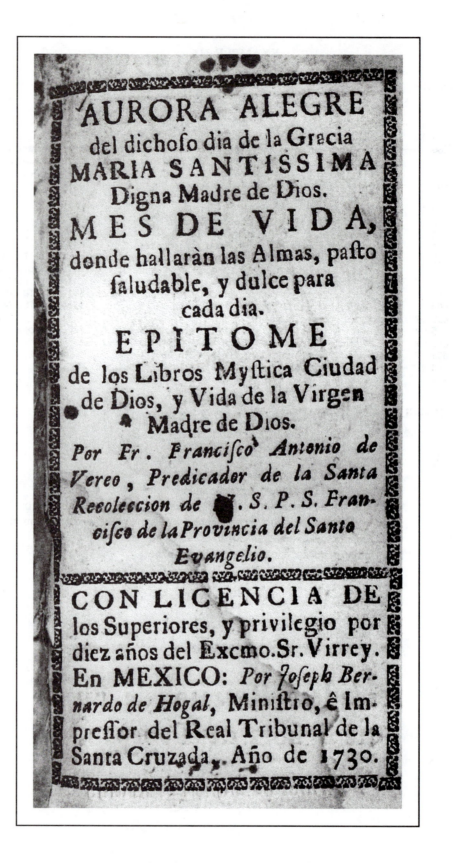

EXAMPLE 32: Title page to vol. 1

EXAMPLE 32

CATALOG RECORD

ref. no.			
	100	1	Vereo, Francisco Antonio de.
1,2,3,4	245	10	Aurora alegre del dichoso dia de la Gracia Maria Santissima digna Madre de Dios : $b mes de vida, donde hallaràn las almas, pasto saludable, y dulce para cada dia : epitome de los libros Mystica ciudad de Dios, y vida de la Virgen Madre de Dios / $c por Fr. Francisco Antonio de Vereo, predicador de la Santa Recoleccion de N.S.P. S. Francisco de la provincia del Santo Evangelio.
5,6,7,8	260		En Mexico : $b Por Joseph Bernardo de Hogal ..., $c año de 1730.
9,10,11	300		2 v. ([42], 769, [73] p.) : $b 1 ill. ; $c 14 cm. (12mo)
12	500		Based on the Mística ciudad de Dios of sor María de Jesús de Agreda.
13	500		Title within ornamental border; woodcut on t.p. verso of v. 1: Verdadero retrato de Nuestra Señora de Tepepan.
14	510	4	Palau y Dulcet (2nd ed.), $c 360017
15	500		Library's copy in old limp vellum, with traces of ties. $5 [INSTITUTION CODE]
	700	0	María de Jesús, $c de Agreda, sor, $d 1602-1665. $t Mística ciudad de Dios.

PRINCIPAL *DCRB* RULES ILLUSTRATED

ref. no.		
1	0H, par. 1	(accents not added to "dia," "Maria," etc.)
2	0K, par. 3	(space between two distinct initialisms)
3	1D2, par. 1	(other titles or phrases following title proper treated as other title information)
4	1G8	(qualifications retained in statement of responsibility)
5	4B2	(words or phrases associated with place name transcribed)
6	4C1	(printer named in publisher statement)
7	4C2	(words or phrases preceding publisher statement transcribed)
8	4D1	(phrase in date transcribed)
9	5D1, par. 3	(format)
10	5B16	(publication in more than one physical unit)
11	5B19	(continuous pagination in publication in more than one physical unit)
12	7C1	(nature, scope or artistic form note)
13	7C10	(physical description note)
14	7C14	(references to published descriptions)
15	7C18	(copy-specific note) See Introduction regarding Local Note Options

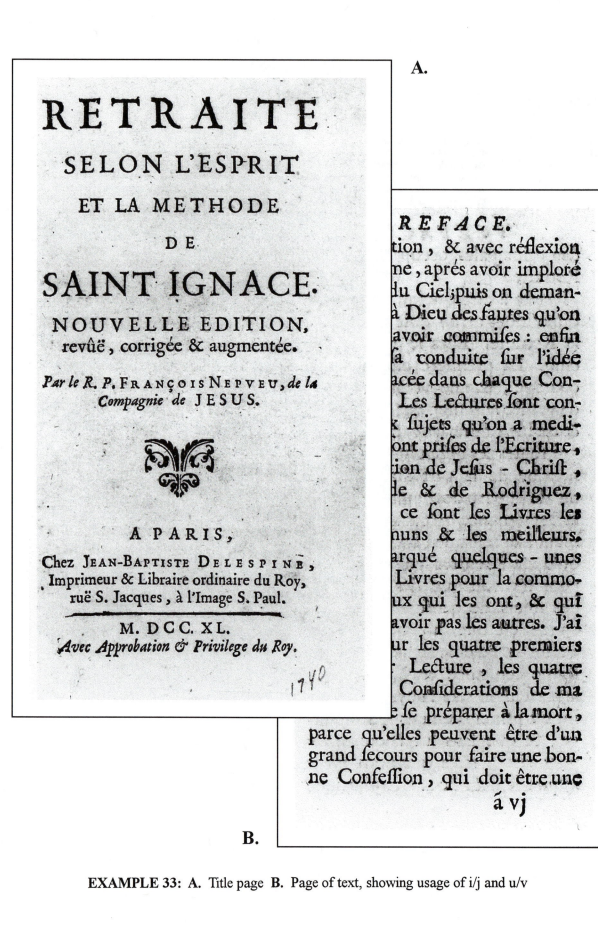

A.

RETRAITE
SELON L'ESPRIT
ET LA METHODE
DE
SAINT IGNACE.
NOUVELLE EDITION,
revûë, corrigée & augmentée.

Par le R. P. François Nepveu, *de la Compagnie de* JESUS.

A PARIS,

Chez Jean-Baptiste Delespine,
Imprimeur & Libraire ordinaire du Roy,
rüe S. Jacques, à l'Image S. Paul.

M. DCC. XL.
Avec Approbation & Privilege du Roy.

1740

B.

REFACE.

...tion , & avec réflexion
...ne , aprés avoir imploré
...du Ciel; puis on deman-
...à Dieu des fautes qu'on
...avoir commises : enfin
...sa conduite sur l'idée
...acée dans chaque Con-
...Les Lectures sont con-
...sujets qu'on a medi-
...ont prises de l'Ecriture,
...tion de Jesus - Christ ,
...de & de Rodriguez ,
...ce sont les Livres les
...muns & les meilleurs.
...arqué quelques - unes
...Livres pour la commo-
...ux qui les ont, & qui
...avoir pas les autres. J'ai
...ur les quatre premiers
...r Lecture , les quatre
...Considerations de ma
...se préparer à la mort ,
parce qu'elles peuvent être d'un
grand secours pour faire une bon-
ne Confession , qui doit être une
á vj

EXAMPLE 33: A. Title page **B.** Page of text, showing usage of i/j and u/v

EXAMPLE 33

CATALOG RECORD

ref. no.

	100 1	Nepveu, François, $d 1639-1708.
1,2,3,4,5	245 10	Retraite selon l'esprit et la methode de Saint Ignace / $c par le R.P. François Nepveu, de la Compagnie de Jesus.
1,2,6,7	250	Nouvelle edition, revûë, corrigée & augmentée.
1,2,8,9,10	260	A Paris : $b Chez Jean-Baptiste Delespine ..., $c 1740.
11,12	300	[22], 352 p. ; $c 17 cm. (12mo)
13	500	The author statement appears on the t.p. after the edition statement.
14	500	Signatures: ã¹²(-ã12) A-O¹² P⁸.
15	500	Initial; head- and tail-pieces.
16	500	From the library of Robert E. Cushman, with his bookplate. $5 [INSTITUTION CODE]
16	500	Bound in full sprinkled calf, gilt-tooled spine, red leather spine label, red sprinkled edges, Jesuit seal on front and back covers with lettering: Tolosani Col. Convic. $5 [INSTITUTION CODE]
	655 7	Devotional literature $z France $y 18th century. $2 rbgenr
	655 7	Sprinkled calf bindings (Binding) $2 rbbin $5 [INSTITUTION CODE]
	655 7	Sprinkled edges (Binding) $2 rbbin $5 [INSTITUTION CODE]
	655 7	Autographs (Provenance) $2 rbprov $5 [INSTITUTION CODE]
	655 7	Bindings (Provenance) $2 rbprov $5 [INSTITUTION CODE]
	655 7	Seals (Provenance) $x Jesuit. $2 rbprov $5 [INSTITUTION CODE]
	700 0	Ignatius, $c of Loyola, Saint, $d 1491-1556. $t Exercitia spiritualia.
17	700 1	Cushman, Robert Earl, $e former owner. $5 [INSTITUTION CODE]
	752	France $d Paris

PRINCIPAL *DCRB* RULES ILLUSTRATED

ref. no.

1	0H, par. 1	(accents not added to "methode", "Jesus," "edition," etc.)
2	0H, par. 3	(convert to uppercase or lowercase according to AACR2; transcribe i/j and u/v according to pattern in main text)
3	0K, par. 1	(initials transcribed without internal spaces)
4	1A2, par. 3	(privilege statement omitted without using mark of omission)
5	1G8	(qualifications retained in statement of responsibility)
6	2B1	(words or phrases associated with edition statement transcribed)
7	2C2	(statement of responsibility appears after edition statement)
8	4B2	(words or phrases associated with place name transcribed)
9	4C2	(words or phrases preceding publisher statement transcribed)
10	4D2, par. 1	(roman numerals in date transcribed as arabic numerals)
11	5B3	(pagination sequence includes unnumbered pages)
12	5D1, par. 3	(format)
13	7C6, par. 4	(statement of responsibility note: name transposed)
14	7C9	(signatures note)
15	7C10	(physical description note)
16	7C18	(copy-specific note) See Introduction regarding Local Note Options
17		See Introduction regarding Local Added Entry Options

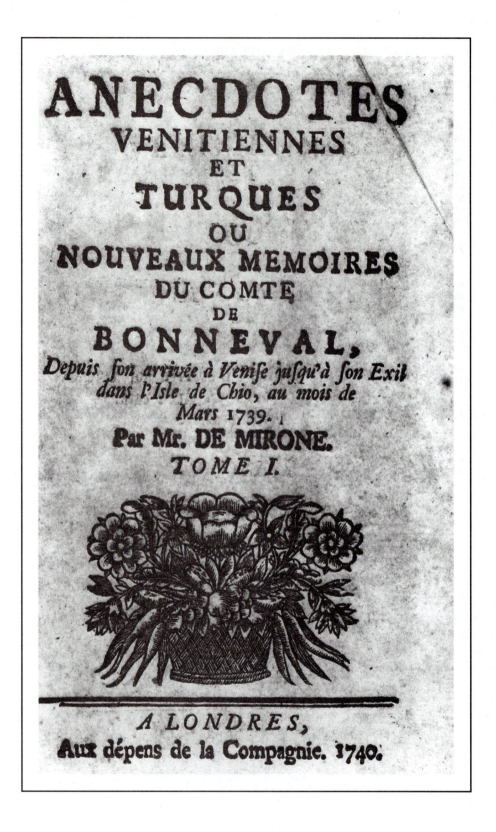

EXAMPLE 34: Title page to vol. 1

EXAMPLE 34

CATALOG RECORD

ref. no.

	100	2	Lambert de Saumery, Pierre, $d b. ca. 1690.
2,3,4,5	245	10	Anecdotes venitiennes et turques, ou, Nouveaux memoires du comte de Bonneval : $b depuis son arrivée à Venise jusqu'à son exil dans l'isle de Chio, au mois de mars 1739 / $c par Mr. de Mirone.
20	246	30	Nouveaux memoires du comte de Bonneval
1,2,6,7,8,9,10	260		A Londres [i.e. Utrecht] : $b Aux dépens de la Compagnie, $c 1740.
11,12,13,14	300		2 v. : $b port. (engraving) ; $c 17 cm. (8vo)
15	500		By Pierre Lambert de Saumery.
16	500		Actual place of publication from Weller. Druckorte.
17	500		Titles in red and black; device on t.p.'s.
17	500		Head- and tail-pieces; initials.
18	510	4	Weller, E.O. Falsche Druckorte, $c II, p. 106
12,19	500		Bound in 1 v., in contemporary full leather, blind-ruled covers, gilt-tooled spine and spine label, marbled endpapers, all edges red. $5 [INSTITUTION CODE]
	655	7	Travel literature. $2 rbgenr
	655	7	False imprints (Publishing) $2 rbpub
	655	7	Blind tooled bindings (Binding) $2 rbbin $5 [INSTITUTION CODE]
	655	7	Marbled papers (Binding) $2 rbbin $5 [INSTITUTION CODE]
	655	7	Stained edges (Binding) $2 rbbin $5 [INSTITUTION CODE]
	752		Netherlands $d Utrecht
	752		England $d London

PRINCIPAL *DCRB* RULES ILLUSTRATED

ref. no.

1	0E, par. 9	(interpolations)
2	0H, par. 1	(accent not added to "memoires")
3	1A2, par. 4	(volume statement omitted without using mark of omission)
4	1B3	(title proper inclusive of alternative title)
5	1G7	(title of address in statement of responsibility)
6	4B1	(place of publication supplied in English form and transcribed as it appears)
7	4B2	(words or phrases associated with place name transcribed)
8	4B9	(fictitious place of publication)
9	4B10	(place of publication supplied from reference source)
10	4C2	(words or phrases preceding publisher statement transcribed)
11	5B16	(publication in more than one physical unit)
12	5B16, par. 3	(issued and bound in different number of volumes)
13	5C1	(illustrations; **option:** describe graphic process or technique)
14	5D1, par. 3	(format)
15	7C6, par. 1	(authorship note)
16	7C8	(publication note)
17	7C10	(physical description note)
18	7C14	(reference to published descriptions)
19	7C18	(copy-specific note) See Introduction regarding Local Note Options
20	App. A.1B3	(added entry for alternative title)

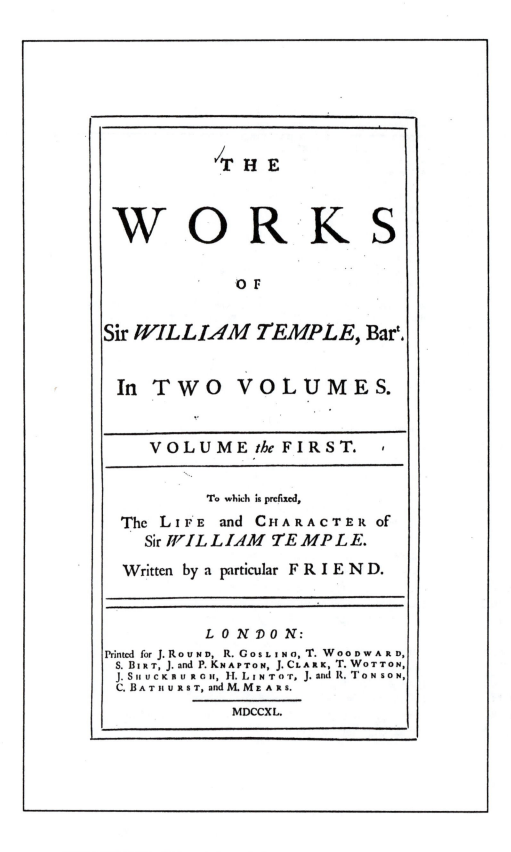

EXAMPLE 35: Title page to vol. 1

EXAMPLE 35

CATALOG RECORD

ref. no.

	100 1	Temple, William, $c Sir, $d 1628-1699.
	240 10	Works. $f 1740
1,2,3,4	245 14	The works of Sir William Temple, bart. : $b in two volumes ... : to which is prefixed, The life and character of Sir William Temple, written by a particular friend.
14	246 3	$i Binder's title: $a Temple's works $5 [INSTITUTION CODE]
4,5,6	260	London : $b Printed for J. Round ... [and 11 others], $c 1740.
7,8	300	2 v. ; $c 36 cm. (fol.)
9	500	Each work has special title page.
9	500	Engraved frontispiece to vol. 1 (portrait of Sir William Temple by G. Vertue after Lely).
10	510 4	ESTC, $c t145994
11	505 0	v. 1. The life and character of Sir William Temple / written by a particular friend [his sister, Lady Martha Giffard]. Observations upon the United Provinces of the Netherlands. Miscellanea. Memoirs, the third part, from the peace concluded 1679 to the time of the author's retirement from publick business. Memoirs of what past in Christendom from the war begun 1672, to the peace concluded 1679 -- v. 2. Letters written by Sir William Temple, bart., and other ministers of state ... from 1665 to 1672 ... / pub. by Jonathan Swift. Letters to the king ... and other persons ... / pub. by Jonathan Swift. An introduction to the history of England.
12	500	Library's copy in old panelled calf, with binder's title: Temple's works; ink inscription ("Charles Steyning, Highden, May 6th 1792") on front fly-leaf of vol. 1. $5 [INSTITUTION CODE]
	700 1	Swift, Jonathan, $d 1667-1745.
	700 12	Giffard, Martha, $c Lady, $d 1638-1722. $t Life and character of Sir William Temple, bart.
15	700 1	Steyning, Charles, $e former owner. $5 [INSTITUTION CODE]
13	740 02	Life and character of Sir William Temple.
	752	England $d London

PRINCIPAL *DCRB* RULES ILLUSTRATED

ref. no.

1	1A1, par. 4	(colon precedes each unit of other title information)
2	1B1	(statement of responsibility inseparably linked to title proper)
3	1D3	(volume/part designation transcribed as other title information)
4	4C2	(words or phrases preceding publisher statement transcribed)
5	4C6, par. 1	(multiple publisher statements; first statement plus [and *x* others])
6	4D2, par. 1	(roman numerals in date transcribed as arabic numerals)
7	5B16	(publication in more than one physical unit)
8	5D1, par. 3	(format)
9	7C10	(physical description note)
10	7C14	(references to published descriptions)
11	7C16	(formal contents note)
12	7C18	(copy-specific note) See Introduction regarding Local Note Options
13	App. A.1E1-2	(added entry for title of additional work)
14	App. A.7C18	(added entry for copy-specific title: binder's title)
15		See Introduction regarding Local Added Entry Options

T. LUCRETIUS CARUS

OF THE

NATURE of THINGS,

IN SIX BOOKS.

ILLUSTRATED with

Proper and Useful NOTES.

Adorned with COPPER-PLATES,

Curiously ENGRAVED

By *GUERNIER*, and others.

Carmina fublimis *tunc funt peritura* Lucreti
Exitio Terras *cum dabit una* Dies.   OVID.

IN TWO VOLUMES.

LONDON:
Printed for DANIEL BROWNE, at the *Black Swan*
without *Temple-Bar.*

MDCCXLIII.

EXAMPLE 36: Title page to vol. 1

EXAMPLE 36

CATALOG RECORD

ref. no.

	100 2	Lucretius Carus, Titus.
	240 10	De rerum natura. $l English & Latin
1,2,3,4,5,6,7	245 10	Of the nature of things : $b in six books / $c T. Lucretius Carus ; illustrated with proper and useful notes ; adorned with copper-plates, curiously engraved by Guernier, and others ; in two volumes.
19	246 3	T. Lucretius Carus Of the nature of things
8,9	260	London : $b Printed for Daniel Browne ..., $c 1743.
10,11	300	2 v. : $b ill. ; $c 21 cm. (8vo)
12	500	Translation of: De rerum natura.
13	546	Latin text and English prose translation on opposite pages.
14	500	Author's name transposed from head of title.
15	500	Illustrations on folded leaves of plates.
16	510 4	ESTC, $c t049793
16	510 4	Gordon, C.A. Lucretius, $c 502B
17	500	Includes indexes.
18	500	From the library of Chester Noyes Greenough and Ruth Hornblower Greenough, with their bookplates. $5 [INSTITUTION CODE]
	655 7	Bookplates (Provenance) $2 rbprov $5 [INSTITUTION CODE]
	700 1	Du Guernier, Louis, $d 1677-1716, $e engraver.
20	700 1	Greenough, Chester Noyes, $d 1874-1938, $e former owner. $5 [INSTITUTION CODE]
20	700 1	Greenough, Ruth Hornblower, $e former owner. $5 [INSTITUTION CODE]
	700 1	Browne, Daniel, $e bookseller.
	752	England $d London
	856 7	$u http://the-tech.mit.edu/Classics/Carus/nature_things.sum.html $2 http

PRINCIPAL *DCRB* RULES ILLUSTRATED

ref. no.

1	1A2, par. 3	(epigram omitted without using mark of omission)
2	1B1	(statement of responsibility separable from title proper; transposed to appropriate area of record)
3	1D3	(volume/part designation transcribed as other title information)
4	1G3	(statement of responsibility transposed without using mark of omission)
5	1G6	(multiple statements of responsibility)
6	1G12	(statement of responsibility without explicitly named person or body)
7 of	1G14, par. 2	(phrase transcribed after statement of responsibility; punctuated as subsequent statement responsibility)
8	4C2	(words or phrases preceding publisher statement transcribed; address omitted)
9	4D2, par. 1	(roman numerals in date transcribed as arabic numerals)
10	5B16	(publication in more than one physical unit)
11	5D1, par. 3	(format)
12	7C2	(language of publication note; translation)
13	7C2	(language of publication note)
14	7C6, par. 4	(statement of responsibility note: name transposed)
15	7C10	(physical description note)
16	7C14	(references to published descriptions)
17	7C16	(informal contents note)
18	7C18	(copy-specific note) See Introduction regarding Local Note Options
19	App. A.1B1	(added entry for title proper, inclusive of transposed elements)
20		See Introduction regarding Local Added Entry Options

Stultus verfus *Sapientem:*

IN THREE

LETTERS

TO THE

FOOL,

ON

SUBJECTS the moft Interefting.

By HENRY FIELDING, Efq;

Joculare tibi videtur : & fane læve,
Dum nihil habemus majus, calamo ludimus.
Sed diligenter intuere has nænias ;
Quantum fubillis utilitatem reperies !

PHÆD.

LONDON: Printed and
DUBLIN Re-printed by E. BATE, in
George's-Lane, 1749.

EXAMPLE 37: Title page

EXAMPLE 37

CATALOG RECORD

ref. no.

	100 1	Fielding, Henry, \$d 1707-1754.
1,2	245 10	Stultus versus Sapientem : \$b in three letters to the fool, on subjects the most interesting / \$c by Henry Fielding, Esq.
3,4,5,6	260	[Dublin] : \$b London printed and Dublin re-printed by E. Bate, in George's-Lane, \$c 1749.
7,8,9	300	23, [1] p. (the last p. blank) ; \$c 17 cm. (8vo)
10	510 4	ESTC, \$c n024312
11	500	From the library of Jerome Kern, with his bookplate. \$5 [INSTITUTION CODE]
	655 7	Letters. \$2 rbgenr
	655 7	Satires. \$2 rbgenr
	655 7	Bookplates (Provenance) \$2 rbprov \$5 [INSTITUTION CODE]
12	700 1	Kern, Jerome, \$d 1885-1945, \$e former owner. \$5 [INSTITUTION CODE]
	752	Ireland \$d Dublin

PRINCIPAL *DCRB* RULES ILLUSTRATED

ref. no.

1	1A2, par. 3	(epigram omitted without using mark of omission)
2	1G7	(title of address in statement of responsibility transcribed)
3	4B8	(place of publication appears only as part of another area; supplied in modern English form)
4	4C1	(printer named in publisher statement)
5	4C2	(words or phrases preceding publisher statement transcribed; address included)
6	4C3	(place of publication transcribed as part of publisher statement)
7	5B3	(pagination sequence includes unnumbered pages)
8	5B7, par. 1	(expansion of statement of extent)
9	5D1, par. 3	(format)
10	7C14	(references to published descriptions)
11	7C18	(copy-specific note) See Introduction regarding Local Note Options
12		See Introduction regarding Local Added Entry Options

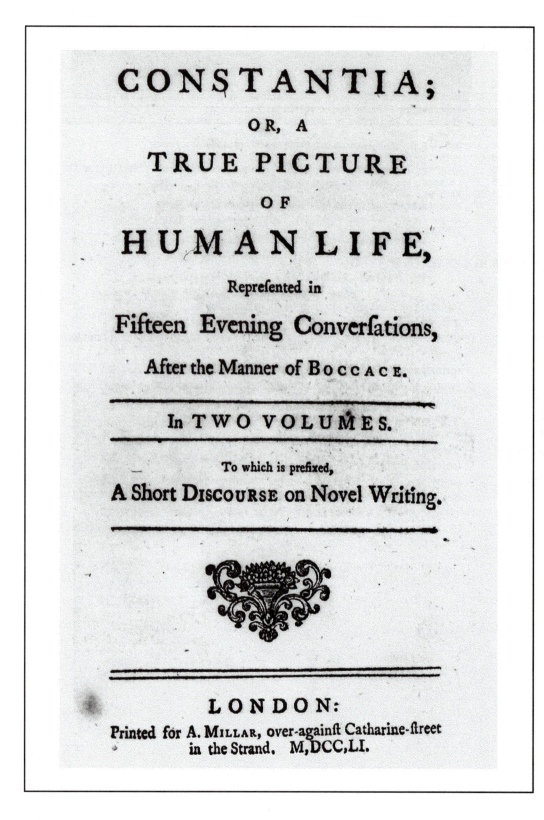

CONSTANTIA;

OR, A

TRUE PICTURE

OF

HUMAN LIFE,

Reprefented in

Fifteen Evening Converfations,

After the Manner of BOCCACE.

In TWO VOLUMES.

To which is prefixed,

A Short DISCOURSE on Novel Writing.

LONDON:

Printed for A. MILLAR, over-againft Catharine-ftreet
in the Strand. M,DCC,LI.

EXAMPLE 38: Title page to vol. 1

EXAMPLE 38

CATALOG RECORD

ref. no.

1,2,3	245 00	Constantia, or, A true picture of human life : $b represented in fifteen evening conversations, after the manner of Boccace : in two volumes : to which is prefixed, A short discourse on novel writing.
11	246 30	Constantia
11	246 30	True picture of human life
4,5	260	London : $b Printed for A. Millar ..., $c 1751.
6,7	300	2 v. ; $c 17 cm. (12mo)
8	500	Head-pieces; initials; press figures.
9	510 4	ESTC, $c n005136
10	500	Bound in gilt-ruled, full sprinkled calf, gilt-tooled red morocco spine labels, red sprinkled edges. $5 [INSTITUTION CODE]
	655 7	Imaginary conversations $y 18th century. $2 rbgenr
	655 7	Press figures (Printing) $2 rbpri
	655 7	Sprinkled calf bindings (Binding) $2 rbbin $5 [INSTITUTION CODE]
	655 7	Sprinkled edges (Binding) $2 rbbin $5 [INSTITUTION CODE]
12	740 02	Short discourse on novel writing.
	752	England $d London

PRINCIPAL *DCRB* RULES ILLUSTRATED

ref. no.

1	1B3	(title proper inclusive of alternative title)
2	1D2, par. 1	(other titles or phrases following title proper treated as other title information)
3	1D3	(volume/part designation transcribed as other title information)
4	4C2	(words or phrases preceding publisher statement transcribed; address omitted)
5	4D2, par. 1	(roman numerals in date transcribed as arabic numerals)
6	5B16	(publication in more than one physical unit)
7	5D1, par. 3	(format)
8	7C10	(physical description note)
9	7C14	(references to published descriptions)
10	7C18	(copy-specific note) See Introduction regarding Local Note Options
11	App. A.1B3	(added entry for alternative title)
12	App. A.1E1-2	(added entry for title of additional work)

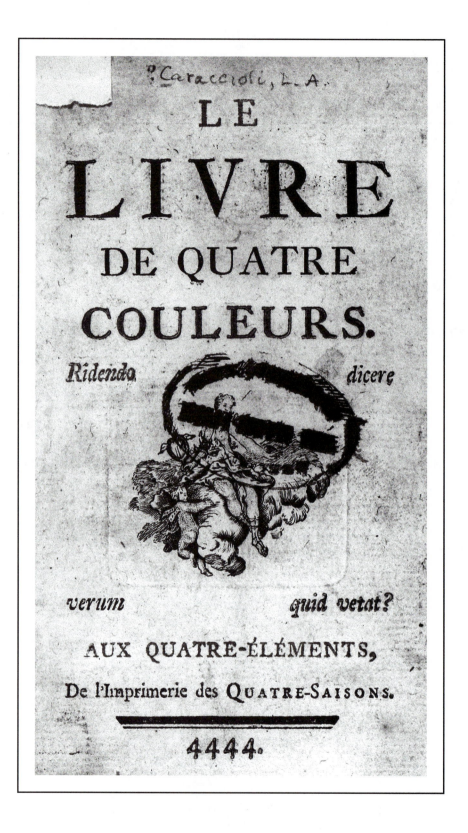

EXAMPLE 39: Title page

EXAMPLE 39

CATALOG RECORD

ref. no.

	100 1	Caraccioli, Louis-Antoine, $c marquis, $d 1719-1803.
2	245 13	Le livre de quatre couleurs.
1,3,4,5	260	Aux Quatre-Éléments : $b De l'imprimerie des quatre-saisons, $c 4444 $a [i.e. Paris : $b Duchesne, $c 1760]
6,7	300	[4], xxiv, 110 p. ; $c 17 cm. (8vo)
8	500	By Louis-Antoine Caraccioli; author and actual imprint supplied from Barbier.
10	500	The text is dated at end "A Paris, ce 3 août, 1757" and reference sources (see below) vary in supplying date.
9	500	NUC pre-1956 cites eds. of 110 and 114 p.
11	500	Signatures: pi² A-H⁸·⁴ I-K⁸ L⁴(-L4, blank).
12	500	Printed in green, brown, red and yellow-orange.
13	510 4	Barbier, A.A. Ouvrages anonymes, $c II, column 1327
13	510 4	Brunet $c III, column 1122
13	510 4	Cioranescu, A. 18. s., $c 15478
13	510 4	Grässe $c II, p. 44
14	500	Library stamp on t.p. cancelled with black ink. $5 [INSTITUTION CODE]
14	500	Ms. bibliographical notice (from Brunet) pasted to front endpaper. $5 [INSTITUTION CODE]
14	500	Bound in paste-paper boards with calf shelfback, hinges broken, spine detached and broken. $5 [INSTITUTION CODE]
	655 7	Fictitious imprints (Publishing) $z France $y 18th century. $2 rbpub
	655 7	Printing in multiple colors (Printing) $z France $y 18th century. $2 rbpri
	752	France $d Paris

PRINCIPAL *DCRB* RULES ILLUSTRATED

ref. no.

1	0E, par. 9	(interpolations)
2	1A2, par. 3	(motto omitted without using mark of omission)
3	4A4	(fictitious imprint; correct imprint supplied from reference source)
4	4C8	(publisher supplied from reference source)
5	4D2, par. 4	(incorrect date transcribed as it appears; corrected date added)
6	5B3	(pagination sequence includes unnumbered pages)
7	5D1, par. 3	(format)
8	7C6, par. 1	(authorship note; source of attribution included)
9	7C7	(edition and bibliographic history note)
10	7C8	(publication note)
11	7C9	(signatures note)
12	7C10	(physical description note)
13	7C14	(references to published descriptions)
14	7C18	(copy-specific note) See Introduction regarding Local Note Options

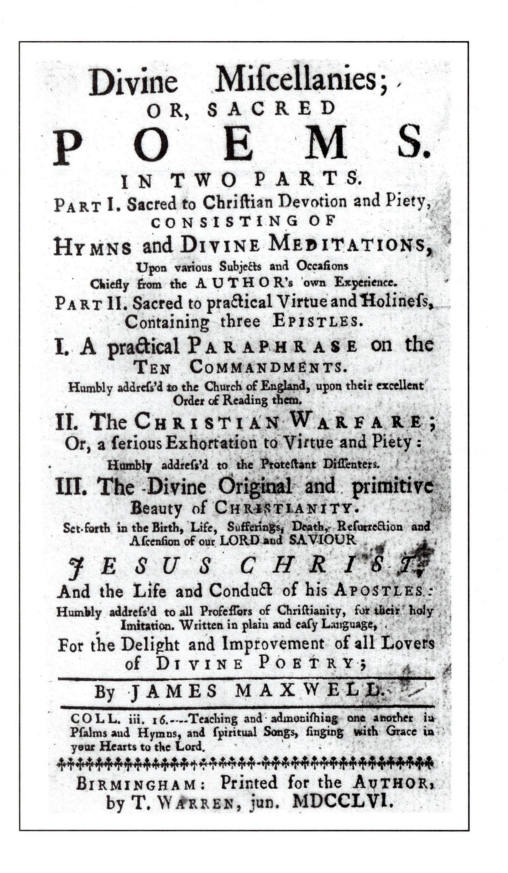

Divine Miscellanies;
OR, SACRED
POEMS.
IN TWO PARTS.

PART I. Sacred to Christian Devotion and Piety,
CONSISTING OF

HYMNS and DIVINE MEDITATIONS,

Upon various Subjects and Occasions
Chiefly from the AUTHOR's own Experience.

PART II. Sacred to practical Virtue and Holiness,
Containing three EPISTLES.

I. A practical PARAPHRASE on the
TEN COMMANDMENTS.

Humbly address'd to the Church of England, upon their excellent
Order of Reading them.

II. The CHRISTIAN WARFARE;
Or, a serious Exhortation to Virtue and Piety:

Humbly address'd to the Protestant Dissenters.

III. The Divine Original and primitive
Beauty of CHRISTIANITY.

Set-forth in the Birth, Life, Sufferings, Death, Resurrection and
Ascension of our LORD and SAVIOUR

JESUS CHRIST,

And the Life and Conduct of his APOSTLES:

Humbly address'd to all Professors of Christianity, for their holy
Imitation. Written in plain and easy Language,

For the Delight and Improvement of all Lovers
of DIVINE POETRY;

By JAMES MAXWELL.

COLL. iii. 16.----Teaching and admonishing one another in
Psalms and Hymns, and spiritual Songs, singing with Grace in
your Hearts to the Lord.

BIRMINGHAM: Printed for the AUTHOR,
by T. WARREN, jun. MDCCLVI.

EXAMPLE 40A: Title page

CATALOG RECORD

ref. no.

	100 1	Maxwell, James, $d 1720-1800.
1,2,3,4	245 10	Divine miscellanies, or, Sacred poems : $b in two parts ... : written in plain and easy language, for the delight and improvement of all lovers of divine poetry / $c by James Maxwell.
16	246 30	Divine miscellanies
16	246 30	Sacred poems
5,6,7	260	Birmingham : $b Printed for the author, by T. Warren, Jun., $c 1756.
8,9,10	300	[28], 324 p., [1] leaf of plates : $b ill. ; $c 17 cm. (12mo)
11	500	Signatures: A^{12} a^2 B-$2E^6$.
12	500	Initials; head- and tail-pieces.
13	500	List of subscribers: p. [3]-[11] (1st group).
16	500	Errata: p. [28] (1st group).
14	504	Includes bibliographical references.
15	505 0	(from t.p.) Part I. Sacred to Christian devotion and piety, consisting of hymns and divine meditations ... -- Part II. Sacred to practical virtue and holiness, containing three epistles. I. A practical paraphrase on the Ten Commandments ... II. The Christian warfare ... III. The divine original and primitive beauty of Christianity ...
	655 7	Devotional literature. $2 rbgenr
	655 7	Errata lists (Printing) $2 rbpri
	655 7	Subscription lists (Publishing) $z England $z Birmingham $y 18th century. $2 rbpub
	752	England $d Birmingham

PRINCIPAL *DCRB* RULES ILLUSTRATED

ref. no.

1	1A2, par. 3	(bible verse omitted without using mark of omission)
2	1B3	(title proper inclusive of alternative title)
3	1D2, par. 2	(other title information constitutes formal statement of contents)
4	1D3	(volume/part designation transcribed as other title information)
5	4C1	(publisher statement includes printer)
6	4C2	(words or phrases preceding publisher statement transcribed)
7	4D2, par. 1	(roman numerals in date transcribed as arabic numerals)
8	5B3	(pagination sequence includes unnumbered pages)
9	5B9	(leaves of plates)
0	5D1, par. 3	(format)
11	7C9	(signatures note)
12	7C10	(physical description note)
13	7C16	(informal contents note)
14	7C16	(informal contents note: mandatory errata leaf note)
15	7C16	(formal contents (from t.p.) note)
16	App. A.1B3	(added entry for alternative title)

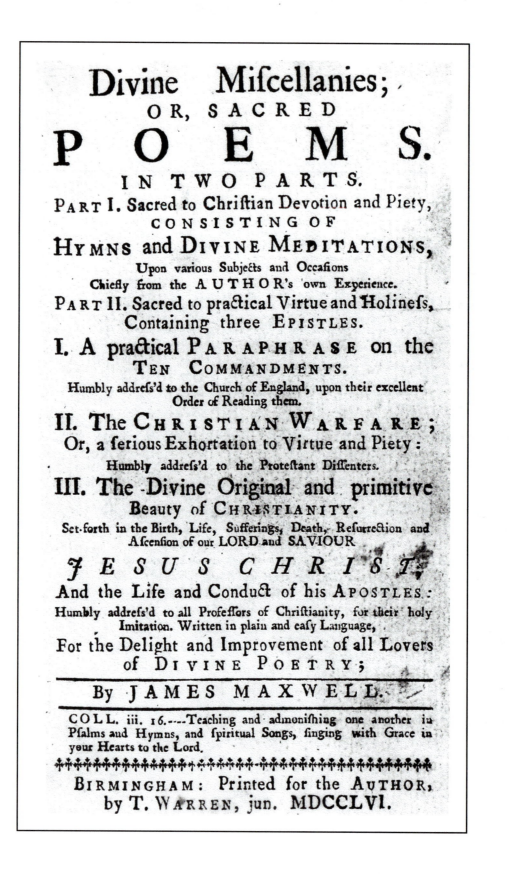

Divine Miscellanies;
OR, SACRED
POEMS.
IN TWO PARTS.

PART I. Sacred to Christian Devotion and Piety,
CONSISTING OF
HYMNS and DIVINE MEDITATIONS,
Upon various Subjects and Occasions
Chiefly from the AUTHOR's own Experience.

PART II. Sacred to practical Virtue and Holiness,
Containing three EPISTLES.

I. A practical PARAPHRASE on the TEN COMMANDMENTS.
Humbly address'd to the Church of England, upon their excellent
Order of Reading them.

II. The CHRISTIAN WARFARE;
Or, a serious Exhortation to Virtue and Piety:
Humbly address'd to the Protestant Dissenters.

III. The Divine Original and primitive Beauty of CHRISTIANITY.
Set-forth in the Birth, Life, Sufferings, Death, Resurrection and
Ascension of our LORD and SAVIOUR

JESUS CHRIST,
And the Life and Conduct of his APOSTLES:
Humbly address'd to all Professors of Christianity, for their holy
Imitation. Written in plain and easy Language,
For the Delight and Improvement of all Lovers
of DIVINE POETRY;

By JAMES MAXWELL.

COLL. iii. 16.----Teaching and admonishing one another in
Psalms and Hymns, and spiritual Songs, singing with Grace in
your Hearts to the Lord.

✳✳✳✳✳✳✳✳✳✳✳✳✳✳✳✳✳✳✳✳✳✳✳✳✳✳✳✳

BIRMINGHAM: Printed for the AUTHOR,
by T. WARREN, jun. MDCCLVI.

EXAMPLE 40B: Title page

MINIMAL-LEVEL CATALOG RECORD, WITHOUT OPTIONS

(App. D: Areas 0-6 and 8 followed, all allowable abridgments made, no mandatory notes made, no notes in area 7 made, title and special files access points omitted)

ref. no.

	100 1	Maxwell, James, $d 1720-1800.
1,2,3,4	245 10	Divine miscellanies, or, Sacred poems : $b in two parts ... / $c by James Maxwell.
5,6,7	260	Birmingham : $b Printed for the author, by T. Warren, Jun., $c 1756.
8,9,10	300	[28], 324 p., [1] leaf of plates : $b ill. ; $c 17 cm. (12mo)

PRINCIPAL *DCRB* RULES ILLUSTRATED

ref. no.

1	1A2, par. 3	(bible verse omitted without using mark of omission)
2	1B3	(title proper inclusive of alternative title)
3	1D3	(volume/part designation transcribed as other title information)
4	1D4	(lengthy other title information abridged)
5	4C1	(publisher statement includes printer)
6	4C2	(words or phrases preceding publisher statement transcribed)
7	4D2, par. 1	(roman numerals in date transcribed as arabic numerals)
8	5B3	(pagination sequence includes unnumbered pages)
9	5B9	(leaves of plates)
10	5D1, par. 3	(format)

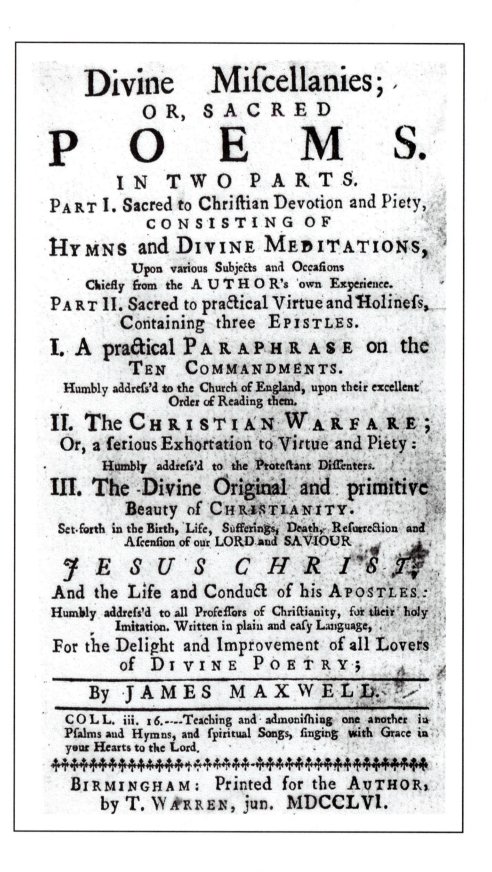

Divine Miscellanies;
OR, SACRED
POEMS.
IN TWO PARTS.

PART I. Sacred to Christian Devotion and Piety,
CONSISTING OF
HYMNS and DIVINE MEDITATIONS,
Upon various Subjects and Occasions
Chiefly from the AUTHOR's own Experience.

PART II. Sacred to practical Virtue and Holiness,
Containing three EPISTLES.

I. A practical PARAPHRASE on the TEN COMMANDMENTS.
Humbly address'd to the Church of England, upon their excellent
Order of Reading them.

II. The CHRISTIAN WARFARE;
Or, a serious Exhortation to Virtue and Piety:
Humbly address'd to the Protestant Dissenters.

III. The Divine Original and primitive Beauty of CHRISTIANITY.
Set-forth in the Birth, Life, Sufferings, Death, Resurrection and
Ascension of our LORD and SAVIOUR
JESUS CHRIST,
And the Life and Conduct of his APOSTLES:
Humbly address'd to all Professors of Christianity, for their holy
Imitation. Written in plain and easy Language,

For the Delight and Improvement of all Lovers
of DIVINE POETRY;

By JAMES MAXWELL.

COLL. iii. 16.----Teaching and admonishing one another in
Psalms and Hymns, and spiritual Songs, singing with Grace in
your Hearts to the Lord.

❋❋❋❋❋❋❋❋❋❋❋❋❋❋❋❋❋❋❋❋❋❋❋❋❋

BIRMINGHAM: Printed for the AUTHOR,
by T. WARREN, jun. MDCCLVI.

EXAMPLE 40C: Title page

MINIMAL-LEVEL CATALOG RECORD, WITH OPTIONS

(App. D: Areas 0-6 and 8 followed, all allowable abridgments made, mandatory notes made, no notes in area 7 made, title and special files access points made)

ref. no.

ref. no.		
	100 1	Maxwell, James, $d 1720-1800.
1,2,3,4	245 10	Divine miscellanies, or, Sacred poems : $b in two parts ... / $c by James Maxwell.
12	246 30	Divine miscellanies
12	246 30	Sacred poems
5,6,7	260	Birmingham : $b Printed for the author, by T. Warren, Jun., $c 1756.
8,9,10	300	[28], 324 p., [1] leaf of plates : $b ill. ; $c 17 cm. (12mo)
11	500	Errata: p. [28] (1st group).
	655 7	Devotional literature. $2 rbgenr
	655 7	Errata lists (Printing) $2 rbpri
	655 7	Subscription lists (Publishing) $z England $z Birmingham $y 18th century. $2 rbpub

PRINCIPAL *DCRB* RULES ILLUSTRATED

ref. no.

ref. no.		
1	1A2, par. 3	(bible verse omitted without using mark of omission)
2	1B3	(title proper inclusive of alternative title)
3	1D3	(volume/part designation transcribed as other title information)
4	1D4	(lengthy other title information abridged)
5	4C1	(publisher statement includes printer)
6	4C2	(words or phrases preceding publisher statement transcribed)
7	4D2, par. 1	(roman numerals in date transcribed as arabic numerals)
8	5B3	(pagination sequence includes unnumbered pages)
9	5B9	(leaves of plates)
10	5D1, par. 3	(format)
11	7C16	(informal contents note: mandatory errata leaf note)
12	App. A.1B3	(added entry for alternative title)

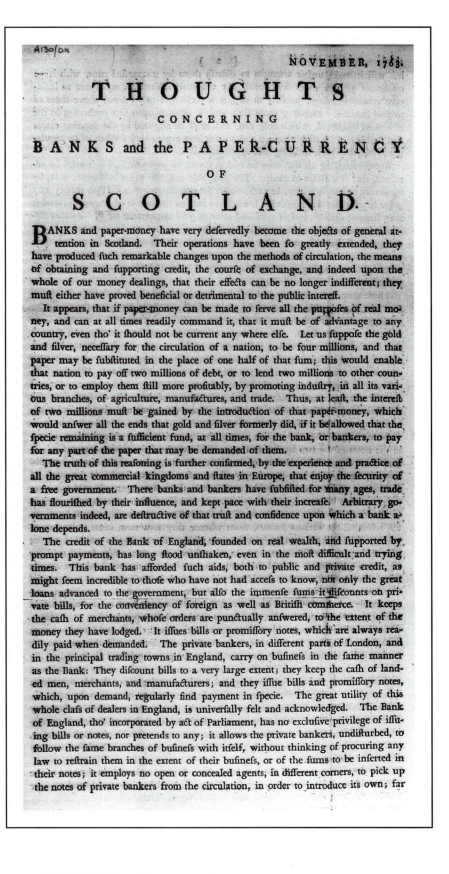

NOVEMBER, 1763.

THOUGHTS

CONCERNING

BANKS and the PAPER-CURRENCY

OF

SCOTLAND.

BANKS and paper-money have very deservedly become the objects of general attention in Scotland. Their operations have been so greatly extended, they have produced such remarkable changes upon the methods of circulation, the means of obtaining and supporting credit, the course of exchange, and indeed upon the whole of our money dealings, that their effects can be no longer indifferent; they must either have proved beneficial or detrimental to the public interest.

It appears, that if paper-money can be made to serve all the purposes of real money, and can at all times readily command it, that it must be of advantage to any country, even tho' it should not be current any where else. Let us suppose the gold and silver, necessary for the circulation of a nation, to be four millions, and that paper may be substituted in the place of one half of that sum; this would enable that nation to pay off two millions of debt, or to lend two millions to other countries, or to employ them still more profitably, by promoting industry, in all its various branches, of agriculture, manufactures, and trade. Thus, at least, the interest of two millions must be gained by the introduction of that paper-money, which would answer all the ends that gold and silver formerly did, if it be allowed that the specie remaining is a sufficient fund, at all times, for the bank, or bankers, to pay for any part of the paper that may be demanded of them.

The truth of this reasoning is further confirmed, by the experience and practice of all the great commercial kingdoms and states in Europe, that enjoy the security of a free government. There banks and bankers have subsisted for many ages, trade has flourished by their influence, and kept pace with their increase. Arbitrary governments indeed, are destructive of that trust and confidence upon which a bank alone depends.

The credit of the Bank of England, founded on real wealth, and supported by prompt payments, has long stood unshaken, even in the most difficult and trying times. This bank has afforded such aids, both to public and private credit, as might seem incredible to those who have not had access to know, not only the great loans advanced to the government; but also the immense sums it discounts on private bills, for the conveniency of foreign as well as British commerce. It keeps the cash of merchants, whose orders are punctually answered, to the extent of the money they have lodged. It issues bills or promissory notes, which are always readily paid when demanded. The private bankers, in different parts of London, and in the principal trading towns in England, carry on business in the same manner as the Bank: They discount bills to a very large extent; they keep the cash of landed men, merchants, and manufacturers; and they issue bills and promissory notes, which, upon demand, regularly find payment in specie. The great utility of this whole class of dealers in England, is universally felt and acknowledged. The Bank of England, tho' incorporated by act of Parliament, has no exclusive privilege of issuing bills or notes, nor pretends to any; it allows the private bankers, undisturbed, to follow the same branches of business with itself, without thinking of procuring any law to restrain them in the extent of their business, or of the sums to be inserted in their notes; it employs no open or concealed agents, in different corners, to pick up the notes of private bankers from the circulation, in order to introduce its own; far

EXAMPLE 41: First page of text

EXAMPLE 41

CATALOG RECORD

ref. no.

	245 00		Thoughts concerning banks and the paper-currency of Scotland.
1,2,3	260		[Scotland : $b s.n.], $c 1763.
4,5	300		3, [1] p. ; $c 39 cm. (fol.)
6	500		Caption title.
7	500		At head of title: November, 1763.
8	510 4		Kress Lib., $c 6144
9		500	Disbound, previously folded in smaller binding, bottom third of inner margin cut away at fold. $5 [INSTITUTION CODE]

PRINCIPAL *DCRB* RULES ILLUSTRATED

ref. no.

1	0E, par. 9	(interpolations)
2	4B12	(probable place of publication supplied from reference source)
3	4C9	(publisher unknown)
4	5B2	(statement of extent for a normally imposed single sheet given in same manner as for a volume)
5	5D1, par. 3	(format)
6	7C3	(source of title proper note)
7	7C8	(publication note)
8	7C14	(references to published descriptions)
9	7C18	(copy-specific note) See Introduction regarding Local Note Options

Exposition Succincte

de

l'Origine et des Progrès

du Peuple qu'on appelle

les Quakers ou les Trembleurs :

Où l'on declare ingenûment leur Principe Fon-
damental, leurs Doctrines, leur Culte, leur
Ministère, et leur Discipline.

Avec un Abregé des précedentes Œconomies ou
Dispensations de Dieu au Monde, par voie d'Introduction.

―――――――――――――――――――

Par GUILLAUME PENN.

―――――――――――――――――――

A quoi l'on a ajouté un des Temoignages rendus
à la Lumiére, par GEORGE FOX.

―――――――――――――――――――

Le Tout traduit de l'*Anglois* par CLAUDE GAY.

―――――――――――――――――――

Comme inconnus : Et toutefois étant reconnus. 2 *Cor.* vi. 9.

Mais il étoit envoyé pour rendre Temoignage à la Lumiére.
Cette Lumiére étoit la veritable, qui illumine tout homme
venant au Monde. *Jean* i. 8, 9.

―――――――――――――――――――

A LONDRES :

Imprimé par LUC HINDE demeurant dans *George-
yard* en *Lombard-street.* 1764.

EXAMPLE 42: Title page

90

EXAMPLE 42

CATALOG RECORD

ref. no.

	100	1	Penn, William, $d 1644-1718.
	240	10	Brief account of the rise and progress of the people called Quakers. $l French
1,2,3,4,5,6,7	245	10	Exposition succincte de l'origine et des progrès du peuple qu'on appelle les quakers ou les trembleurs : $b où l'on declare ingenûment leur principe fondamental, leurs doctrines, leur culte, leur ministère, et leur discipline : avec un abregé des précedentes œconomies ou dispensations de Dieu au monde, par voie d'introduction / $c par Guillaume Penn ; a quoi l'on a ajouté un des temoignages rendus à la lumière, par George Fox ; le tout traduit de l'anglois par Claude Gay.
1,8,9,10,11	260		A Londres : $b Imprimé par Luc Hinde ..., $c 1764.
12,13,14	300		iv, 109, [3] p. ; $c 20 cm. (8vo)
15	500		Translation of: A brief account of the rise and progress of the people called Quakers.
16	500		Signatures: A-O⁴ P².
17	500		"Instruction pour tous ceux qui voudront connoître le chemin du royaume [par] George Fox": p. [89]-109.
18	500		Errata: p. [2] (3rd group).
19	500		Quarter bound in marbled boards, red sprinkled edges. $5 [INSTITUTION CODE]
	655	7	Quarter bindings (Binding) $2 rbbin $5 [INSTITUTION CODE]
	655	7	Sprinkled edges (Binding) $2 rbbin $5 [INSTITUTION CODE]
	700	1	Gay, Claude, $d 1707?-1786, $e tr.
	700	12	Fox, George, $d 1624-1691. $t To all that would know the way to the kingdom. $l French.
	700	1	Hinde, Luke, $d fl. 1750-1767, $e printer.
20	740	02	Instruction pour tous ceux qui voudront connoître le chemin du royaume.
	752		England $d London

PRINCIPAL *DCRB* RULES ILLUSTRATED

ref. no.

1	0H, par. 1	(accents not added to "declare," "temoignages," etc.)
2	0H, par. 2	(transcribe French ligature as single character)
3	1A1, par. 4	(colon precedes each unit of other title information)
4	1A2, par. 3	(epigram omitted without using mark of omission)
5	1D2, par. 1	(other titles or phrases following title proper treated as other title information)
6	1G6	(multiple statements of responsibility)
7	1G14, par. 2	(phrase transcribed after statement of responsibility; punctuated as subsequent statement of responsibility)
8	4B1	(place of publication transcribed as it appears)
9	4B2	(words or phrases associated with place name transcribed)
10	4C1	(printer named in publisher statement)
11	4C2	(words or phrases preceding publisher statement transcribed; address omitted)
12	5B3	(pagination sequence includes unnumbered pages)
13	5B4	(errata leaf included in statement of extent)
14	5D1, par. 3	(format)
15	7C2	(language of publication note; translation)
16	7C9	(signatures note)
17	7C16	(informal contents note)
18	7C16	(informal contents note: mandatory errata leaf note)
19	7C18	(copy-specific note) See Introduction regarding Local Note Options
20	App. A.1E1-2	(added entry for title of additional work)

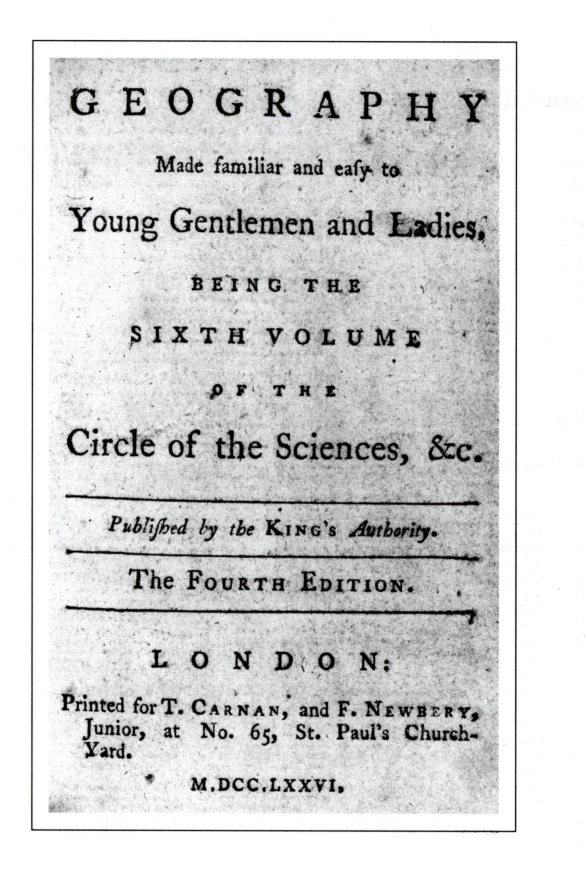

GEOGRAPHY

Made familiar and easy to

Young Gentlemen and Ladies,

BEING THE

SIXTH VOLUME

OF THE

Circle of the Sciences, &c.

Published by the KING's *Authority.*

The Fourth Edition.

LONDON:

Printed for T. CARNAN, and F. NEWBERY, Junior, at No. 65, St. Paul's Church-Yard.

M.DCC.LXXVI.

EXAMPLE 43: Title page

EXAMPLE 43

CATALOG RECORD

ref. no.

	245 00	Geography made familiar and easy to young gentlemen and ladies : $b being the sixth volume of The circle of the sciences, &c.
1	250	The fourth edition.
2,3	260	London : $b Printed for T. Carnan, and F. Newbery, Junior ..., $c 1776.
4,5,6	300	[20], 319, [13] p. ; $c 11 cm. (32mo in 8s)
8	500	Edited by John Newbery. Cf. Osborne Coll., I, p. 133.
9	500	First published in 1748 by John Newbery. Cf. NUC pre-1956 416:653.
10	500	"Published by the King's authority."
11	500	Signatures: A-Y^8.
12	500	Roscoe records no definite information on the presence of a folding map, which is present in the first ed. No copies of the fourth ed. with a map are recorded.
14	500	Integral publisher's ads: [13] p. at end.
13	510 4	ESTC, $c t112043
13	510 4	Roscoe, S. John Newbery, $c J63(4)
14	500	From the library of Elisabeth Ball. $5 [INSTITUTION CODE]
14	500	Bound in original blue boards, damaged, with green vellum shelfback; printed paper label on spine. $5 [INSTITUTION CODE]
	700 1	Newbery, John, $d 1713-1767.
16	700 1	Ball, Elisabeth, $d 1897-1982, $e former owner. $5 [INSTITUTION CODE]
7	830 0	Circle of the sciences ; $v v. 6.
	752	England $d London

PRINCIPAL *DCRB* RULES ILLUSTRATED

ref. no.

1	2B1	(words or phrases associated with edition statement transcribed)
2	4C2	(words or phrases preceding publisher statement transcribed; address omitted)
3	4D2, par. 1	(roman numerals in date transcribed as arabic numerals)
4	5B3	(pagination sequence includes unnumbered pages)
5	5B5	(leaves/pages of advertisments included in statement of extent)
6	5D1, par. 3	(format)
7	6	(series in pre-1801 work)
8	7C6, par. 1	(authorship note; source of attribution included)
9	7C7	(edition and bibliographic history note)
10	7C8	(publication note)
11	7C9	(signatures note)
12	7C10	(physical description note)
13	7C14	(references to published descriptions)
14	7C16	(informal contents note; advertisements)
15	7C18	(copy-specific note) See Introduction regarding Local Note Options
16		See Introduction regarding Local Added Entry Options

No. 26.

LES SABATS

JACOBITES.

Inutilité et danger des Clubs.

LE mal est fait, il faut se résigner et le supporter : que ne puis-je dire y porter remède ! Je le dirois peut-être si ces assemblées d'hommes, que des circonstances difficiles ont fait naître, n'étoient pas devenues le foyer de la licence. A l'aurore de la liberté, quand la constitution n'existoit pas ; il étoit naturel que chacun s'occupât du sort qu'il pouvoit espérer, des dangers qu'il avoit à redouter, des vertus qu'il devoit acquérir et des loix qu'il faudroit observer; il n'etoit pas étonnant que chacun voulût s'en entretenir, et puiser dans le commerce de ses semblables les lumières et la patience.

Aujourd'hui la constitution est faite, le sort de tous les habitans de la France est à-peu-près fixé : ceux, qui sont encore dans l'incertitude

A 2

EXAMPLE 44: Page 3 of issue no. 26

EXAMPLE 44

CATALOG RECORD

ref. no.

	100 1	Marchant, François, $d 1761-1793.
	245 14	Les sabats jacobites.
1,9	260	[Paris] : $b J. Blanchon, $c -1792.
2,3	300	3 v. : $b ill. ; $c 22 cm. (8vo)
	362 1	Began in 1791.
	362 0	-no 75.
4,10	500	Description based on: No 26; title from caption.
5	500	By François Marchant. Cf. NUC pre-1956 513:105.
6	500	Place of publication from publisher-supplied volume t.p.
	515	No 26-no 50 called t. 2; no 51-no 75 called t. 3e.
7	510 4	Martin & Walter. Cat. de la Révolution française, $c V, p. 1306
8	500	Bound in blue pasteboard, edges untrimmed. $5 [INSTITUTION CODE]
9	500	Bound with v. 3 is the author's Les grands sabats, pour servir de suite aux Sabats jacobites. $5 [INSTITUTION CODE]
	655 7	Pasteboard (Binding) $2 rbbin $5 [INSTITUTION CODE]
	785 00	Marchant, François, $d 1761-1793. $t Grands sabats, pour servir de suite aux Sabats jacobites $w (OCoLC) 10461385 $w (DLC)sc 84008709
	752	France $d Paris

PRINCIPAL *DCRB* RULES ILLUSTRATED

ref. no.

1	0E, par. 9	(interpolations)
2	5B16	(publication in more than one physical unit)
3	5D1, par. 3	(format)
4	7C3	(source of title proper note)
5	7C6, par. 1	(authorship note; source of attribution included)
6	7C8	(publication note)
7	7C14	(references to published descriptions)
8	7C18	(copy-specific note) See Introduction regarding Local Note Options
9	7C19	(copy-specific "with:" note) See Introduction regarding Local Note Options
10	App. C.1.4	(rare serials: information supplied from source other than prescribed source of information)

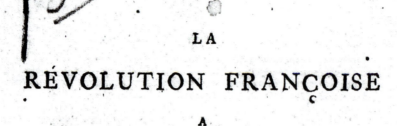

LA

RÉVOLUTION FRANÇOISE

A

GENÈVE;

TABLEAU

HISTORIQUE ET POLITIQUE

DE

LA CONDUITE DE LA FRANCE
ENVERS LES GENEVOIS,

DEPUIS LE MOIS D'OCTOBRE 1792, AU MOIS D'OCTOBRE
1794.

Veluti in Speculo.

LONDRES:

De l'Imprimerie de T. SPILSBURY & FILS.

Se vend chez P. ELMSLEY, *Strand;* J. DEBRETT,
Piccadilly; & J. DE BOFFE, *Gerrard-Street, Soho.*

EXAMPLE 45: Title page

EXAMPLE 45

CATALOG RECORD

ref. no.

	100 1	Ivernois, Francis d', \$c Sir, \$d 1757-1842.
2,3	245 13	La Revolution françoise a Genève : \$b tableau historique et politique de la conduite de la France envers les genevois, depuis le mois d'octobre 1792, au mois d'octobre 1794.
1,4,5,6,7,8	260	Londres : \$b De l'imprimerie de T. Spilsbury & fils : \$b Se vend chez P. Elmsley ..., J. Debrett ..., & J. De Boffe ..., \$c [1794 or 1795]
9	300	75, [1] p. ; \$c 22 cm.
10	500	Written by Francis d'Ivernois. Cf. NUC pre-56, v. 274, p. 256.
11	500	Signatures: [A]^2 B-K^4 L^2.
12	500	Printed on wove paper.
12	500	Press figures.
13	500	Imperfect copy: leaf L2 (p. 75-[76]) lacking. \$5 [INSTITUTION CODE]
	655 7	Chronicles. \$2 rbgenr
	655 7	Wove papers (Paper) \$z France \$y 18th century. \$2 rbpap
	655 7	Press figures (Printing) \$2 rbpri
	752	England \$d London

PRINCIPAL *DCRB* RULES ILLUSTRATED

ref. no.

1	0E, par. 9	(interpolations)
2	0H, par. 1	(accent not added to "Revolution")
3	1A2, par. 3	(epigram omitted without using mark of omission)
4	4B1	(place of publication transcribed as it appears)
5	4C1	(publisher statement includes printer and booksellers)
6	4C2	(words or phrases preceding publisher statement transcribed; addresses omitted)
7	4C6, par. 1	(multiple publishers separated by prescribed punctuation)
8	4D6	(date uncertain; "one year or the other" pattern used)
9	5B3	(pagination sequence includes unnumbered pages)
10	7C6, par. 1	(authorship note; source of attribution included)
11	7C9	(signatures note)
12	7C10	(physical description note)
13	7C18	(copy-specific note) See Introduction regarding Local Note Options

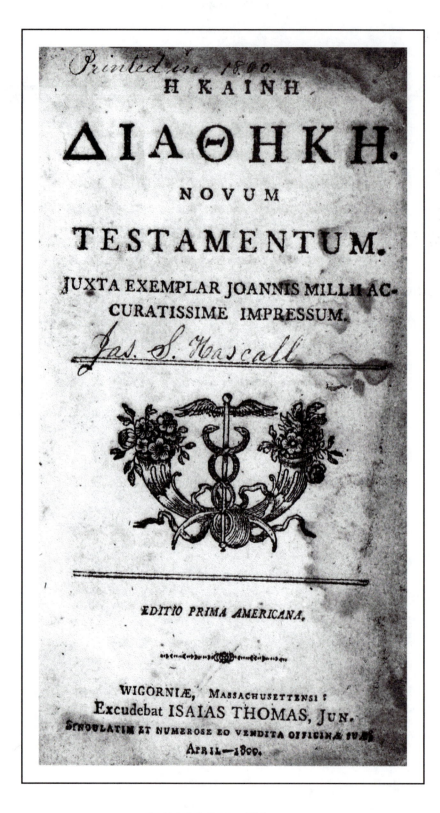

EXAMPLE 46: Title page

98

EXAMPLE 46

CATALOG RECORD

ref. no.

	130	0	Bible. $p N.T. $l Greek. $s Mill. $f 1800.
3,4	245	13	Hē Kainē Diathēkē = $b Novum Testamentum / $c juxta exemplar Joannis Millii accuratissime impressum.
18	246	31	Novum Testamentum
5	250		Editio prima Americana.
1,2,3,4,7,8, 9	260		Wigorniae [Worcester], Massachusettensi : $b Excudebat Isaias Thomas, Jun. sinoulatim [i.e. singulatim] et numerose eo vendita officina suae, $c April 1800.
10,11	300		478, [2] p. ; $c 18 cm. (12mo)
12	500		Greek text in double columns.
12	500		First three words in Greek characters on t.p.
13	500		Edited by Caleb Alexander. Cf. p. [3].
14	500		Signatures: A-2R⁶.
15	510	4	Evans, $c 36952
16	500		Advertising matter on final leaf.
17	| 500		Bound in contemporary full leather, gilt-tooled spine and red leather spine label. $5 [INSTITUTION CODE]
17	| 500		From the library of Jas. S. Hascall, with his signature. $5 [INSTITUTION CODE]
	700	1	Mill, John, $d 1645-1707.
	700	1	Alexander, Caleb, $d 1655 7-1828, $e ed.
	700	1	Thomas, Isaiah, $c Jun., $d 1773-1819, $e printer.
19	| 700	1	Hascall, Jas. S., $e former owner. $5 [INSTITUTION CODE]
	752		United States $b Massachusetts $d Worcester

PRINCIPAL *DCRB* RULES ILLUSTRATED

ref. no.

1	0G	(misprint transcribed as it appears)
2	0H, par. 2	(transcribe Latin ligature as component letters)
3	0H, par. 3	(convert to uppercase or lowercase according to AACR2; transcribe i/j and u/v according to pattern in main text)
4	1C	(title proper inclusive of parallel title)
5	2B1	(words or phrases associated with edition statement transcribed)
6	4B1	(place of publication transcribed as it appears)
7	4B3	(modern form of place name added)
8	4C1	(printer/bookseller named in publisher statement)
9	4D1	(month in date transcribed)
10	5B5	(leaves/pages of advertisement included in statement of extent)
11	5D1, par. 3	(format)
12	7C2	(language of publication note)
13	7C6, par. 2	(other statements of responsibility note)
14	7C9	(signatures note)
15	7C14	(references to published descriptions)
16	7C16	(informal contents note: advertisements)
17	7C18	(copy-specific note) See Introduction regarding Local Note Options
18	App. A.7C4-5	(added entry for parallel title)
19		See Introduction regarding Local Added Entry Options

B.

GAZETTEER,

OR

GEOGRAPHICAL DICTIONARY,

OF

NORTH AMERICA AND THE WEST INDIES,

CONTAINING

I.—A GENERAL DESCRIPTION OF NORTH AMERICA. II.—A GENERAL DESCRIPTION OF THE UNITED STATES; THE DECLARATION OF INDEPENDENCE AND CONSTITUTION OF THE UNITED STATES. III.—A DESCRIPTION OF ALL THE STATES, COUNTIES, CITIES, TOWNS, VILLAGES, FORTS, SEAS, HARBORS, CAPES, RIVERS, LAKES, CANALS, RAIL-ROADS, MOUNTAINS, &c.

CONNECTED WITH NORTH AMERICA;

WITH THE EXTENT, BOUNDARIES AND NATURAL PRODUCTIONS OF EACH STATE; THE BEARING AND DISTANCE OF REMARKABLE PLACES FROM EACH OTHER AND OF EACH FROM THE CITY OF WASHINGTON, WITH THE POPULATION ACCORDING TO THE CENSUS OF 1830.

CONTAINING

LIKEWISE MANY TABLES RELATING TO THE COMMERCE, POPULATION, REVENUE, DEBT, AND VARIOUS INSTITUTIONS OF THE UNITED STATES.

COMPILED FROM THE MOST RECENT AND AUTHENTIC SOURCES

BY BISHOP DAVENPORT.

Baltimore:
PUBLISHED BY GEORGE M'DOWELL & SON.

1833.

A.

EXAMPLE 47: A. Title page **B.** Title page verso

EXAMPLE 47

CATALOG RECORD

ref. no.		field	content
		100 1	Davenport, Bishop.
1		245 12	A new gazetteer, or geographical dictionary, of North America and the West Indies ... : $b compiled from the most recent and authentic sources / $c by Bishop Davenport.
15	|	246 30	Gazetteer, or geographical dictionary, of North America and the West Indies ... $5 [INSTITUTION CODE]
2,3		260	Baltimore : $b Published by George M'Dowell & Son, $c 1833.
4,5,6,7		300	471, [1] p. (last p. blank), [2] folded leaves of plates : $b ill., maps ; $c 23 cm.
8		500	"Stereotyped by J. Howe"--t.p. verso.
8		500	A variant of the edition described by Checklist Amer. imprints, with "sources" spelled correctly on t.p.
3,9		500	Copyright entered 1832 (t.p. verso).
10		500	Signatures: [A]⁴ B-U⁴ V⁴ W⁴ X-2U⁴ 2V⁴ 2W⁴ 2X-3I⁴.
11		500	Hand-colored maps of North America and the United States engraved by Young & Delleker.
11		500	Some wood engravings by R.S. Gilbert; one possibly cut by William Mason.
12		510 4	Checklist Amer. imprints $c 18500
12		510 4	Thomson, T.R. Railroads, $c 719
12		510 4	Hamilton, S. Amer. book illustrators (1968 ed.), $c 1021
13		505 0	(from t.p.) I. A general description of North America -- II. A general description of the United States; the Declaration of Independence and Constitution of the United States -- III. A description of all the states, counties, cities, towns, villages, forts, seas, harbors, capes, rivers, lakes, canals, rail-roads, mountains, &c. connected with North America ...
14	|	500	Library's copy imperfect: "A new" is cut from the top of the title page; inscribed: Joseph Thorne. $5 [INSTITUTION CODE]
		655 7	Gazetteers. $2 rbgenr
		655 7	Maps $z North America. $2 rbgenr
		700 1	Gilbert, Reuben S., $e wood-engraver.
		700 1	Mason, William, $d fl. 1808-1844, $e wood-engraver.
		710 2	Young & Delleker, $e engraver.
		700 1	Howe, Jonathan, $e stereotyper.
16	|	700 1	Thorne, Joseph, $e former owner. $5 [INSTITUTION CODE]
		710 2	George M'Dowell & Son, $e publisher.
		752	United States $b Maryland $d Baltimore

PRINCIPAL *DCRB* RULES ILLUSTRATED

ref. no.

1	1D2, par. 2	(other title information constitutes formal statement of contents)
2	4C2	(words or phrases preceding publisher statement transcribed)
3	4D2, footnote 8	(copyright date)
4	5B3	(pagination sequence includes unnumbered pages)
5	5B7, par. 1	(expansion of statement of extent)
6	5B9	(leaves of plates)
7	5B10	(folded leaves)
8	7C7	(edition and bibliographic history note)
9	7C8	(publication note)
10	7C9	(signatures note)
11	7C10	(physical description note)
12	7C14	(references to published descriptions)
13	7C16	(formal contents (from t.p.) note)
14	7C18	(copy-specific note) See Introduction regarding Local Note Options
15	App. A.7C18	(added entry for copy-specific title)
16		See Introduction regarding Local Added Entry Options

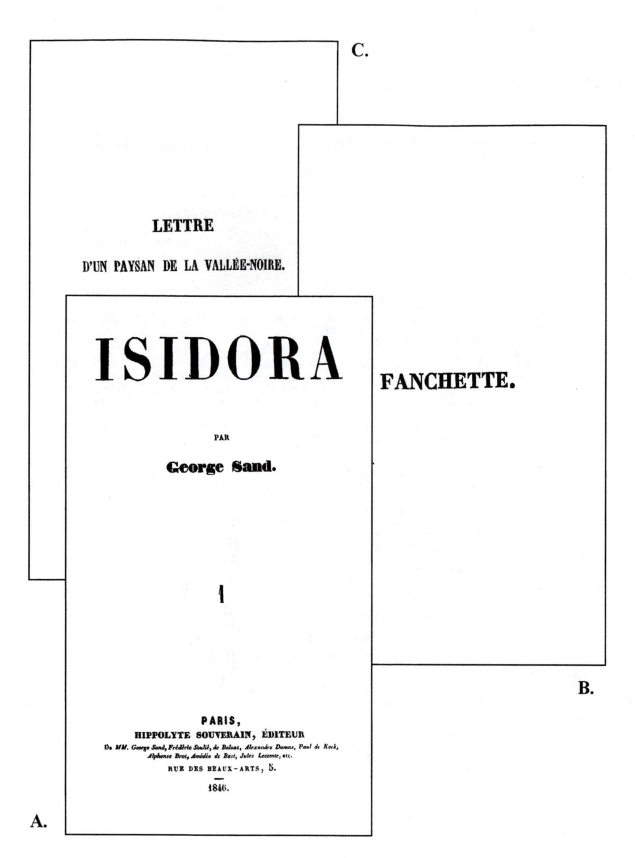

C.

LETTRE

D'UN PAYSAN DE LA VALLÉE-NOIRE.

ISIDORA

FANCHETTE.

PAR

George Sand.

1

PARIS,
HIPPOLYTE SOUVERAIN, ÉDITEUR
De MM. George Sand, Frédéric Soulié, de Balzac, Alexandre Dumas, Paul de Kock,
Alphonse Brot, Amédée de Bast, Jules Lecomte, etc.
RUE DES BEAUX-ARTS, 5.
1846.

A.

B.

EXAMPLE 48: A. Title page to vol. 1 **B–C.** Section titles of works not listed on title page

EXAMPLE 48

CATALOG RECORD

ref. no.

		100 1	Sand, George, $d 1804-1876.
1,2		245 10	Isidora / $c par George Sand.
		260	Paris : $b Hippolyte Souverain ..., $c 1846.
3,4,5		300	3 v. (314, [2]; 309, [3]; 307 [i.e. 297], [3] p.) ; $c 21 cm.
6		500	First authorised edition; first published in 1845. Cf. Colin.
7		500	Pagination error in v. 3: p. 232 is followed by [3] p., pagination resumes with no. 246.
9		500	Vol. 3 also includes the author's Fanchette (p. [87]-232) and Lettre d'un paysan de la Vallée-Noir (p. [233]-307).
8		510 4	Colin, G. George Sand, $c p. 70-72.
8		510 4	Vicaire, G. Livres du 19. s., $c VII, 227-228
10	|	500	Copy 1 with the inkstamp of the Bibliothèque de Tsarskoe Selo. $5 [INSTITUTION CODE]
10	|	500	Copy 2 from the library of George Sand. $5 [INSTITUTION CODE]
10	|	500	Copy 1 bound in green half sheep and marbled boards, edges sprinkled. $5 [INSTITUTION CODE]
10	|	500	Copy 2 bound in two vols., uniformly with other author's copies in purple half morocco and marbled boards, edges marbled; spines numbered as vols. 41-42 of Sand's copies of her works; bookplate of H. Grandjean. $5 [INSTITUTION CODE]
	|	655 7	Authors' copies (Provenance) $z France $y 19th century $2 rbprov $5 [INSTITUTION CODE]
		700 12	Sand, George, $d 1804-1876. $t Fanchette.
		700 12	Sand, George, $d 1804-1876. $t Lettre d'un paysan de la Vallée-Noir.
12	|	700 1	Sand, George, $d 1804-1876, $e former owner. $5 [INSTITUTION CODE]
11		740 02	Fanchette.
11		740 02	Lettre d'un paysan de la Vall´ee-Noir.
		752	France $d Paris

PRINCIPAL *DCRB* RULES ILLUSTRATED

ref. no.

1	1A2, par. 4	(volume statement omitted without using mark of omission)
2	1E2	(additional works not listed on title page)
3	5B6	(multiple sequences of numbering)
4	5B16	(publication in more than one physical unit)
5	5B20	(**option:** pagination of individual volumes given in parentheses after number of units)
6	7C7	(edition and bibliographic history note)
7	7C10	(physical description note)
8	7C14	(references to published descriptions)
9	7C16	(informal contents note)
10	7C18	(copy-specific note) See Introduction regarding Local Note Options
11	App. A.1E1-2	(added entry for title of additional work)
12		See Introduction regarding Local Added Entry Options

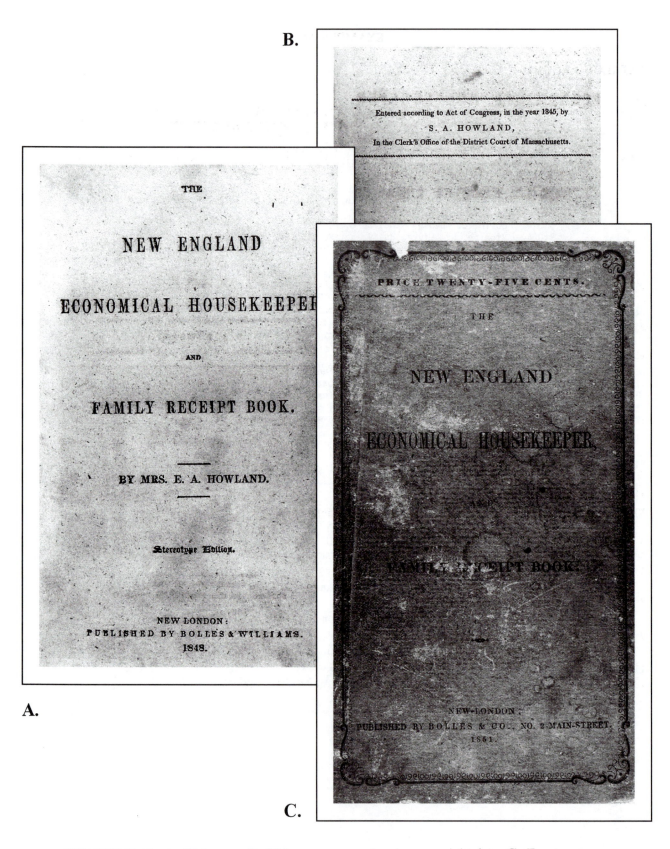

EXAMPLE 49: A. Title page **B.** Title page verso, showing copyright date **C.** Front cover, showing date of impression (images reduced 65 percent)

EXAMPLE 49

CATALOG RECORD

ref. no.

		100 1	Howland, E. A. $q (Esther Allen), $d 1801-1860.
		245 14	The New England economical housekeeper and family receipt book / $c by Mrs. E.A. Howland.
		250	Stereotype edition.
1,2,3		260	New London [Conn.] : $b Published by Bolles & Williams, $c 1848 (1851 impression)
4		300	[6], 11-108 p. : $b ill. ; $c 18 cm.
5		500	First published 1844. See Bitting, Kelly & Wheaton, cited below.
6		500	Cover-title imprint dated 1851.
7		510 4	Bitting, K.G. Gastronomic bib., $c 236
7		510 4	Kelly & Wheaton. Bib. of culinary history, $c 3040-3050
8		500	Publisher's ads on lower board.
9		500	Includes index.
10	|	500	Newspaper recipes pasted in at front, and on first blank at end. $5 [INSTITUTION CODE]
10	|	500	With the bookplate of Mrs. John T. Gernon. $5 [INSTITUTION CODE]
		752	United States $b Connecticut $d New London

PRINCIPAL *DCRB* RULES ILLUSTRATED

ref. no.

1	0E, par. 9	(interpolations)
2	4C2	(words or phrases preceding publisher statement transcribed)
3	4E	(date of impression)
4	5B3	(pagination sequence includes unnumbered pages)
5	7C7	(edition and bibliographic history note)
6	7C8	(publication note)
7	7C14	(references to published descriptions)
8	7C16	(informal contents note; advertisements)
9	7C16	(informal contents note)
10	7C18	(copy-specific note) See Introduction regarding Local Note Options

CHARLES DE GAULLE

LE FIL
DE L'ÉPÉE

GRAVURES AU BURIN

LBERT DECARIS

JUSTIFICATION DU TIRAGE

Le tirage de cette édition a été limité à 450 exemplaires sur vélin de Rives, dont : 5 exemplaires, numérotés de 1 à 5, auxquels on a ajouté une double-planche gravée et encrée, un dessin original double-page, une gravure refusée, une suite sur Auvergne et une suite sur soie de toutes les gravures; 15 exemplaires, numérotés de 6 à 20, auxquels on a ajouté une planche gravée et encrée, un dessin original, une gravure refusée, une suite sur Auvergne de toutes les gravures et le tirage sur soie du frontispice et des cinq planches doubles; 55 exemplaires, numérotés de 21 à 75, auxquels on a ajouté une gravure refusée, une suite sur Auvergne de toutes les gravures et le tirage sur soie du frontispice; 375 exemplaires, numérotés de 76 à 450. Il a été imprimé en outre 25 exemplaires hors-commerce, qui ont été justifiés de I à XXV.

EXEMPLAIRE N° 448

ACHEVÉ D'IMPRIMER LE CINQ DÉCEMBRE MIL NEUF CENT SOIXANTE-TROIS PAR DOMINIQUE VIGLINO POUR LE TEXTE ET PAR JACQUES RIGAL POUR LES GRAVURES.

L LUBINEAU, ÉDITEUR
A PARIS

EXAMPLE 50: A. Title page **B.** Page [4], showing limitation statement **C.** Colophon

EXAMPLE 50

CATALOG RECORD

ref. no.

	100 1	Gaulle, Charles de, $d 1890-1970.
2	245 13	Le fil de l'épée / $c Charles de Gaulle ; gravures au burin d'Albert Decaris.
1,3,4,5	260	A Paris : $b Marcel Lubineau, éditeur, $c [5 Dec. 1963]
6	300	188, [8] p. : $b ill. ; $c 35 cm.
7	500	Author's name transposed from head of title.
8	500	"Le tirage de cette ´edition a été limité à 450 exemplaires sur v´elin de Rives ... Il a été imprimé en outre 25 exemplaires hors-commerce, qui ont été justifiés de I à XXV"--p. [4].
9	500	Date of publication from colophon: Achevé d'imprimer le cinq décembre mil neuf cent soixante-trois par Dominique Viglino pour le texte et par Jacques Rigal pour les gravures.
10	500	In loose quires, issued in a portfolio within a protective case.
11	500	Library has copy no. 448. $5 [INSTITUTION CODE]
	655 7	Livres d'artistes. $2 rbgenr
	655 7	Limitation statements (Publishing) $2 rbpub
	700 1	Decaris, Albert.
	752	France $d Paris

PRINCIPAL *DCRB* RULES ILLUSTRATED

ref. no.

1	0E, par. 9	(interpolations)
2	1G3	(statement of responsibility transposed without using mark of omission)
3	4B2	(words or phrases associated with place name transcribed)
4	4D1	(day and month in date transcribed)
5	4D2, par. 3	(very long verbal date statement transcribed as formalized date)
6	5B3	(pagination sequence includes unnumbered pages)
7	7C6, par. 4	(statement of responsibility note: name transposed)
8	7C7	(edition and bibliographic history note)
9	7C8	(publication note)
10	7C10	(physical description note)
11	7C18	(copy-specific note) See Introduction regarding Local Note Options

RULE INDEX

GENERAL RULES

0B2	Imperfect copy; no reliable description of missing text available, ex. 19
0C3	No title page
	title supplied from reference source, ex. 1
0D	Prescribed sources of information for single-sheet publication, ex. 27
0E, par. 5	**Option:** Double punctuation, ex. 26B
0E, par. 9	Interpolations, ex. 1, 5, 8-9, 15, 19, 22-23, 27-28, 34, 39, 41, 44-45, 49-50
0E, par. 12	Virgule transcribed as comma, ex. 17
0G	Misprint transcribed as it appears, ex. 23, 46
	Missing guide letter supplied in transcription, ex. 2
0H, par. 1	Accents not added, ex. 13, 19, 29, 32-34, 42, 45
0H, par. 2	Ligatures
	French ligature, ex. 42
	Latin ligature, ex. 6, 8, 12, 16, 23, 25, 28, 30, 46
0H, par. 3	Capitalization, transcription of i/j and u/v, ex. 6-8, 11-17, 19-20, 23, 25, 28, 33, 46
0H, par. 4	Capital I (=ii) not converted to lowercase, ex. 21
0H, par. 5	Gothic capitals J and U treated as I and V, ex. 3-4, 6, 17
0J2	Contractions and abbreviations expanded to full form, ex. 3, 5-9
0K, par. 1	Initials transcribed without internal spaces, ex. 21, 29, 33
0K, par. 3	Space between two distinct initialisms, ex. 29, 32

TITLE AND STATEMENT OF RESPONSIBILITY AREA

1A1, par. 4	Colon used before each unit of other title information, ex. 15, 26A-26B, 35, 42
1A2, par. 3-4	Words or phrases omitted without using marks of omission
	bible verse, ex. 16, 40A-40C
	epigram, ex. 29, 31, 36-37, 42, 45
	motto, ex. 39
	privilege statement, ex. 6-7, 29, 33
	volume statement, ex. 34, 48
1B1	Statement of responsibility
	linked to title proper, ex. 3-8, 12, 14-15, 20-21, 25, 28, 30, 35
	separable from title proper, ex. 36
1B3	Title proper inclusive of alternative title, ex. 14, 23, 27, 29, 34, 38, 40A-40C
1B4	Volume designations transcribed as part of title proper, ex. 11
1B5	Titles
	devised from content of work, ex. 18
	taken from opening words of text, ex. 2
1B7	Lengthy titles
	abridged, ex. 5
	lengthy author statement preceding chief title abridged, ex. 28
	qualifications retained in integral author statement, ex. 28, 30
1C	Parallel titles, ex. 28, 46
1D2, par. 1	Other titles or phrases following title proper, ex. 6, 9, 14, 25, 32, 38, 42
1D2, par. 2	Other title information as formal statement of contents, ex. 40A, 47
1D3	Volume/part designation transcribed as other title information, ex. 35-36, 38, 40A-40C
1D4	Lengthy other title information abridged, ex. 28-29, 40B-40C
1D5	Other title information includes statements of responsibility, ex. 3, 14, 25

PHYSICAL DESCRIPTION AREA

SERIES AREA

NOTE AREA

APPENDICES

TITLE INDEX

TITLE INDEX

TITLE INDEX

NAME INDEX

NAME INDEX

TOPICAL INDEX

Note: Terms in parentheses refer to rules.

A

Autographs (7C18), ex. 5, 9, 22, 31, 33, 35, 46-47
Avant-titre, *see* Other title information

B

Bible verse in title page transcription (1A2, par. 3), ex. 40A-40C
Bibliographic citations, etc.
 for incunabula (7C14), ex. 1-2
 in notes (7C14), ex. 1-5, 8-9, 12, 14-17, 22-23, 26A-27, 30-32, 34-39, 41, 43-44, 46-49
Bibliographic description
 additions, *see* Words or phrases
 of work based on imperfect copy (0B2, 5B12, 7C18), ex. 19
Bibliographic history notes (7C7), ex. 2, 9, 22, 26A-26B, 39, 43, 47-50
Bindings and binders (7C10, 7C18), ex. 1-2, 6-7, 9, 11-14, 16-18, 20-24, 26A-26B, 29, 31-35, 38-39, 41-44, 46, 48, 50
Blank leaves or pages
 mentioned in statement of extent (5B3), ex. 37, 47
 mentioned in note (7C10), ex. 11-12, 39
Bookseller in publisher statement (4C1), ex. 24-28, 31, 45-46
Broadsheets, *see* Single-sheet publications
Broadsides, *see* Single-sheet publications

C

Calendars and date(s) of publication, etc.
 Julian (4D2, par. 6), ex. 15
 non-Christian-era (4D2, par. 5), ex. 10
 Roman-style (4D2, par. 5), ex. 2, 4
Capitalization of i/j and u/v (0H, par. 3), ex. 6-8, 11-17, 19-20, 23, 25, 28, 33, 46
 not converted (0H, par. 4), ex. 21
Capitals, Gothic, transcription of (0H, par. 5), ex. 3-4, 6, 17
Caption title (1B3), ex. 41
Chi, use of, in signatures note (7C9), ex. 2
Chief title, added entry for (App. A.1B1), ex. 3, 7-8, 11-12, 14, 20-21, 25, 28, 30
Chronograms (4D2, par. 2), ex. 23
Citations, bibliographic, *see* Bibliographic citations, etc.
Collational formula, optional use of, (7C9), ex. 15
Collections
 of varying character
  publication, etc., area (4A6), ex. 18
 with different imprints (4A6), ex. 18
 without collective title
  added entries (App. A), ex. 48
  punctuation between titles of parts (1E1), ex. 12
  transcribing individual titles (1E1), ex. 12
  recording titles of works not named on t.p. (1E2), ex. 48
  use of "with" notes when parts are cataloged separately (7C19), ex. 3-4
 without meaningful title, option to devise title (1E2), ex. 18
Collective title, devised for collections (1E2), ex. 18
Colon, with other title information (1A1, par. 4), ex. 15, 26A-26B, 35, 42

D

J

L

M

N

on statements of responsibility (1G3, 7C6), ex. 2, 16, 23-24, 27, 33-34, 36, 39, 43-46, 50

on statements of responsibility transposed to precede edition statement (2C2, 7C6, par. 4), ex. 33

on supplied place of publication (4B10, 4B12), ex. 1, 5, 22-23, 34, 41

on title proper (0C3, 1B4-1B5, 7C3), ex. 1-2, 11, 18, 41, 44
    single-sheet publications (1F2), ex. 27

on translations (7C2), ex. 11, 13, 19, 25, 36, 42

on transposition of data (1B1, 1G3, 2C2, 7C6, par. 4, 7C7), ex. 17, 33, 36, 50

on true attribution to a person in presence of incorrect data (7C6), ex. 16, 23, 34

on uniform title in "with" note (7C19), ex. 3-4

on unpublished or miscellaneous collections (4A6), ex. 18

on variant publisher statements in multipart or multivolume items (4C7, 7C8), ex. 29

on variations in title (1B4, 7C4), ex. 7, 11, 16, 20, 27

on volumes as bound (5B16, 7C18), ex. 29, 34

optional, *see* Optional notes

"with" notes, *see* "With" notes

see also Contents notes; Mandatory notes; Optional notes; "With" notes

Number of columns, *see* Columns, number of

Number of lines, *see* Lines, number of

O

œ (French ligature), transcribed as single character (0H, par. 2), ex. 42

Office held, omitted from statement of responsibility (1G8), ex. 28

Omission, marks of

    in publisher statement (4C2, 4C6), ex. 9-10, 13, 19-20, 24, 29, 31-33, 35-36, 38, 42-43, 45

    with omissions from statement of responsibility (1G8), ex. 16, 24-25, 28-29

    with omissions from title proper (1B7), ex. 28

    with omitted contents information from title and statement of responsibility area (1D2, par. 2), ex. 40A, 47

    with omitted other title information (1D4), ex. 29, 40B-40C

    with supplied phrase in English in publisher statement (4C6), ex. 35

Opening words of text, *see* Incipit

Optional notes

    giving full collation (7C9), ex. 15

    on additional imprint information (4A2), ex. 3

    on bindings and binders (7C10, 7C18), ex. 1-2, 6-7, 9, 11-14, 16-18, 20-24, 26A-26B, 29, 31-35, 38-39, 41-44, 46, 48, 50

    on blank leaves or pages (5B7-5B8, 7C10), ex. 2, 11-12, 39

    on chronograms (4D2, par. 2), ex. 23

    on contents, *see* Contents notes

    on copy numbers (7C7, 7C18), ex. 50

    on edition and bibliographic history of item (7C7), ex. 2, 4, 9, 22, 26A-26B, 39, 43-44, 47-50

    on extent (5B20, 7C10), ex. 11, 43, 48

    on illustrations (7C10, 7C18), ex. 17, 23, 32, 35-36, 47, 50

    on imperfections in copies (7C18), ex. 2, 10, 12, 17, 19, 23, 25, 29, 41, 45, 47

    on library's holdings (7C18), ex. 1-2, 5-7, 9-14, 16-17, 20-26B, 29, 31-39, 41-50

    on multiple sequences of leaves or pages (5B20), ex. 11, 48

    on nature, scope, or artistic form of item (7C1), ex. 9, 18, 27-29, 32

    on original position of transposed elements (1G3, 2C2, 7C6, par. 4, 7C7), ex. 23, 33, 36, 50

    on other title information (1D4, 1G14), ex. 28

    on pagination of publication in more than one physical unit (5B20), ex. 11, 48

P

Q

R

S

s (letter), transcribed in modern form (App. B), ex. 3-7, 9, 11, 13-17, 19-20, 23-32, 34, 36-38, 40A-40C, 42-43

"s.n.", use of (4C9), ex. 5, 23, 41

Sections of items, punctuation between

    preceding each unit of other title information (1A1?), ex. 15, 26A-26B, 35, 42

    preceding each subsequent statement of responsibility (1A1), ex. 15, 26A-26B, 35, 42

    with titles of parts by same person(s) or body (bodies) (1E1), ex. 12

Serials (App. C), ex. 44

Sheets, *see* Single-sheet publications

"sic", use of (0G), ex. 23

Sign, Tironian, treated as abbreviation (0J2), ex. 3, 5-6

Signatures (gatherings) (7C9), ex. 2-10, 12-17, 19-26B, 30-31, 33, 39-40A, 42-43, 45-47

    signed with unavailable characters (7C9), ex. 2, 6, 16, 19, 23, 25

Sine nomine (s.n.) (4C9), ex. 5, 23, 41

Single-sheet publications (1F)

    extent (5B2, 5B15), ex. 27, 41

    normally imposed single sheets (5B2), ex. 41

    prescribed source of information (0D), ex. 27

    size (5D5), ex. 27

Size

    multivolume set, different volume heights (5D3), ex. 18

    single-sheet publications (5D5), ex. 27

Space, use of between titles of parts (1E1), ex. 12

Spelling

    gothic capitals (0H, par. 5), ex. 3-4, 6, 17

    i and j (0H, par. 3), ex. 6-8, 11-17, 19-20, 23, 25, 28, 33, 46

        not converted (0H, par. 4), ex. 21

    u, v and w (0H, par. 3), ex. 6-8, 11-17, 19-20, 23, 25, 28, 33, 46

Square brackets, use of (0E)

    with abbreviation "s.n." (4C9), ex. 5, 23, 41

    with adjacent expansions or supplied words (0J2), ex. 3, 5-9

    with corrected extent information (5B7, par. 1), ex. 37, 47

    with corrected publication details (4B9, 4C3), ex. 15, 27-28, 34, 37

    with corrections to misprints (0G), ex. 23, 46

    with devised title (1B5), ex. 18

    with formalized date(s) of publication (4D2, par. 3), ex. 50

    with interpolations (0E, par. 9), ex.1, 5, 8-9, 15, 19, 22-23, 27-28, 34, 39, 41, 44-45, 49-50

    with mark of omission showing lacunae in source of information (0B2), ex. 19

    with supplied alternative form of name or place in publication (4B3), ex. 10, 46

    with supplied arabic numerals for unnumbered leaves or pages (5B3, 5B8), ex. 2-5, 7, 9-10, 12-13, 15-16, 19-20, 22, 24, 26A-26B, 28, 30-31, 33, 37, 39-40C, 42-43, 45-47, 49-50

    with supplied date(s) of publication, etc. (4D5-4D6), ex. 1, 5, 27, 45

    with supplied descriptive terms in signatures notes (7C9), ex. 2, 16, 19, 23, 25

    with supplied letters, in signatures note (7C9), ex. 47

    with supplied letters in place of contractions (0J2), ex. 3, 6-9

    with supplied letters in place of symbols, etc., in signatures note (7C9), ex. 6

    with supplied name of publisher (4C4, 4C8), ex. 1, 8, 22, 39

    with supplied, or combined, publication information (4A2), ex. 1-6, 9

    with supplied phrase in English indicating omission of publishers' names (4C6, par. 1), ex. 35

    with supplied place of publication (4A4, 4B8, 4B10, 4B12), ex. 1, 5, 15, 22-23, 27-28, 34, 37, 39, 41

T

option to transcribe title information to show actual wording of t.p. (7C4), ex. 7, 11, 16, 20, 27

see also Added title pages; Engraved title page; Illustrated title page

Title proper (1B)

    abridgment (1B7), ex. 5

    added entries for (App. A.1B1), ex. 36

    and chief title (1B1, 1B7), ex. 3-8, 12, 14, 20-21, 25, 28, 30

    and parallel titles (1C), ex. 28, 46

    numeration within (1B4), ex. 11

    serials (App. C.1.4), ex. 44

    single-sheet publications (1F), ex. 27

    transcribed in "with" note (7C19), ex. 3-4, 44

Titles

    alternative (1B3, 1B7), ex. 14, 23, 27, 29, 34, 38, 40A-40C

    copy-specific, added entries for (App. A.7C18), ex. 26A-26B, 35, 47

    parallel, *see* Parallel title

    subordinate, *see* Other title information

    subsidiary, *see* Other title information

Titles of additional works, *see* Other title information; Additional titles

Titles of honor, nobility, address, etc., in statement of responsibility (1B7, 1G7), ex. 3-4, 19, 29-31, 34, 37

Transcription of title, *see* Inseparably linked data; Title proper; Transposition of data

Translations (7C2), ex. 11, 13, 19, 25, 36, 42

Transposition of data

    edition statement and statement of responsibility (2C2), ex. 33

    generally not indicated by marks of omission (1A2), ex. 6-7, 16, 29, 31, 33-34, 36-37, 39, 40A-40C, 42, 45

    noting original position of elements and/or areas on t.p. (1B1, 1G3, 2C2, 7C6-7C7), ex. 33, 36, 50

    title proper and other titles or other title information (1B3), ex. 14, 23, 27, 29

    title proper and statement of responsibility (1G3), ex. 36, 50

U

u (letter), transcribed as v (0H, App. A-B), ex. 4, 6

Uniform titles, option to transcribe in "with" note (7C19), ex. 3-4

Unnumbered pages or leaves

    in foliation sequence (5B3), ex. 9-10, 13, 15

    in pagination sequence (5B3, 5B8), ex. 3-4, 12, 16, 19-20, 22, 24, 26A-26B, 28, 30-31, 33, 37, 39-40C, 42-43, 45-47, 49-50

V

v (letter), transcribed as u (0H, App. B), ex. 3, 5-6, 9, 11, 15-17, 23

Vignettes not regarded as illustrations (5C1, 7C10), ex. 30

Virgule, transcription of when used as comma (0E, par. 12), ex. 17

Volumes/parts, number of (1A2, 1D3, 5B16-5B17, 5B20)

    issued and bound in different number of volumes (5B16, par. 3), ex. 29, 34

    pagination (5B20), ex. 11, 48

    publication of in more than one physical unit (5B16), ex. 1, 11, 18, 29, 32, 34-36, 38, 44, 48

    statement of omitted (1A2, par. 3-4), ex. 34, 48

transcribed as other title information (1D3), ex. 35-36, 38, 40A-40C
transcribed as part of title proper (1B4), ex. 11

W

w (letter), transcribed as vv (0H), ex. 20
Width (of volume), *see* Size
"With" notes (7C19), ex. 3-4, 44
Woodcuts
 as part of extent (5C1), ex. 4
 in physical description note (7C10), ex. 5, 17, 32, 47
Words or phrases
 as supplied title (1B5, 1E2), ex. 2, 18
 explanatory
  with edition statement (2B1), ex. 13, 19, 21, 24-25, 30, 33, 43, 46
  with place of publication (4B2), ex. 2-4, 9-11, 13, 15, 17, 19-20, 29, 32-34, 42, 50
  with publisher statement (4C2, 4C6), ex. 2-4, 6, 9-17, 19-21, 24, 26A-38, 40A-40C, 42-43, 45, 47, 49
 in single-sheet publications (1F2), ex. 27
 omitted without using marks of omission (1A2, par. 3-4)
  bible verse, ex. 16, 40A-40C
  epigram, ex. 29, 31, 36-37, 42, 45
  motto, ex. 39
  privilege statement, ex. 6-7, 29, 33
  volume statement, ex. 34, 48
 on t.p. notes, appendices, etc., in work (1G14, par. 2), ex. 17, 22, 24, 36, 42
 option to devise title for collection without meaningful title (1E2), ex. 18
 option to transcribe as they appear in date of publication (4D1), ex. 2-4, 6-7, 9-10, 15, 17, 19-20, 25, 32, 46, 50
 with name of principal place of publication (4B2), ex. 2-4, 9-11, 13, 15, 17, 19-20, 29, 32-34, 42, 50
 with statements of responsibility (1G7-1G8, 1G14, par. 2), ex. 3-4, 16-17, 19, 21-22, 24-26B, 28-34, 37, 41
Wove paper
 in physical description note (7C10), ex. 45